Ying Ying was born to Chinese parents and grew up in Hong Kong. She gained her first degree from the University of Hong Kong in 1980 majoring in English Literature and Chinese Literature. After having worked for the Hong Kong government educating the public against corruption, she completed a Masters course in Criminology. She taught Sociology and Criminal Justice at universities in Hong Kong before she and her family migrated to Australia in 1999. Ying Ying has written two books in Chinese, published in 1992 and 2009 in Hong Kong. *Starting with Max* is her first book in English. She lives in Sydney with her German husband and grown-up daughter.

# STARTING WITH
# MAX.

*How a wise stray dog gave me strength and inspiration*

## YING YING

ALLEN&UNWIN
SYDNEY · MELBOURNE · AUCKLAND · LONDON

First published in Australia in 2013

Allen & Unwin

83 Alexander Street
Crows Nest NSW 2065
Australia
Phone:  (61 2) 8425 0100
Fax:     (61 2) 9906 2218
Email:  info@allenandunwin.com
Web:    www.allenandunwin.com

Cataloguing-in-Publication details are available from the
National Library of Australia
www.trove.nla.gov.au

ISBN 978 1 74331 794 5

Typeset in 11/17pt Minion Pro by Midland Typesetters, Australia
Printed and bound in Australia by McPherson's Printing Group

10 9 8 7 6 5 4 3 2 1

MIX
Paper from
responsible sources
FSC® C001695

The paper in this book is FSC® certified.
FSC® promotes environmentally responsible,
socially beneficial and economically viable
management of the world's forests.

*For Max, more than a dog*

# CONTENTS

## A TIME FOR REFLECTION

# A
# NEW FAMILY
# MEMBER

## CHAPTER ONE

# THE ENCOUNTER

From the first moment I saw Four-Legs I was captivated by his big brown eyes, staring intently at us. They were full of obvious anxiety and seemed to make a silent plea for mercy.

He sat quietly in the middle kennel as we entered the 'Strays' section. I couldn't tell what sort of dog he was, as I'd never seen a dog like him, even in pictures. He was definitely a cross, maybe even of more than two breeds. In the midst of the deafening barking from the dogs around us, his stillness made him seem unreal, like a living statue. But there was something particular about those eyes: they were huge, round and bright, peering up with an eagerness to make contact, showing his desperate longing for a connection and his readiness to begin again. I'd never seen eyes so expressive; they had the ability to demand a response from anyone. 'Who could abandon such eyes?' I asked myself.

Although he remained quiet he was fully alert, the perky ears constantly checking out the changing scene, ready to react to whatever the situation demanded. He moved forward, looked around, wagged his tail, then sat down again in a naturally elegant posture. There was not the slightest sign of the agitation normally found in a stray dog. He seemed to know without making a fuss how clearly he stood out. Then, as we were passing by, he turned his face towards us and smiled. It was this smile that stopped us from leaving.

Even though I knew nothing about dogs, I understood at once that this was a friendly greeting. The lips were drawn back a little, so that the cheeks were pushed upwards to form a soft expression below the eyes, and the mouth was slightly open to show the teeth as the fat tongue half stuck out. My sixth sense told me that some contact was now inevitable—the kind of pre-destined inevitability that I'd always hated.

My heart started to blame my daughter. Why had Ka-ching begged us to come here to see these poor creatures, on such a beautiful Sunday? At the same time I regretted that I hadn't thought twice before I'd made that life-changing promise of a pet while we were still in Hong Kong. I looked up at the blue sky, but the bright sunlight blinded my vision, so I lowered my eyes and checked the expressions on the faces of my dear family. A hot flush suddenly rose from my lower spine: was this the burning sensation of feeling trapped?

As soon as we'd left home that morning for the RSPCA, I'd started secretly praying for a leisurely family outing, just to see some dogs and cats and nothing more, a 'fun' trip, certainly not a 'destiny-altering' excursion during which we would make decisions vital to our future Australian life. I'd also prayed that we were not going to meet any suitable canine candidates. 'Not today,' I'd told myself, 'it shouldn't be today. No, not yet.' I was confused enough by my totally new Sydney environment and I felt fear rising inside me. I simply wasn't ready.

I was relieved when Ka-ching made no requests as we were browsing through the 'For Adoption' section, where a number of good-looking dogs were on display. None of these was what we'd imagined as a potential new member of our family: they were mostly small dogs, unsuitable to guard our house, and the bigger ones were mixed Australian breeds we'd never seen in Hong Kong. We were prepared to take either a labrador or a golden retriever, but that, today, was not meant to be our luck—or so I thought.

We'd next looked at the cats, many of which were lovely, but Ka-ching had been promised a dog. After a few minutes I said, 'That's it,' and was about to suggest going home. It was then that my daughter spotted the 'Strays' section and dragged us over to it.

This was where dogs found lost or abandoned in the streets were kept, usually for only seven days since there was not enough room to keep them longer. According to the RSPCA staff these animals were not supposed to be for adoption, as their backgrounds were unknown and they might have unforeseeable behavioural problems. This was exactly what I wanted to hear.

I was reluctant to follow my daughter, but I told myself, 'There won't be a dog worth adopting here—there's no harm in just taking a look.' Little did I know that one single look would change my life forever.

As we walked closer to greet him, I wondered how such a smart-looking dog could be found among the strays. He was still sitting down but a ray of excitement had rushed into his eyes, and as our eyes met something passed from him to me: a passion, a sort of yearning for dependence, perhaps also inexplicable delight. Somehow my heart was touched, and in that moment it told me I couldn't escape.

The boxer in the very last kennel put his front paws against the fence and barked, scaring a small child, who was quickly carried away by his mother. The bull-terrier next to us raised his voice, yelling for justice, as he glared defiance at anyone passing by. The German shepherd on my left howled in desperation and kept turning around, ready to attack, and I heard a weeping sort of sound from the labrador puppy opposite. She, too, had expressive, bulging eyes that were begging for mercy. The cattle dog kept moving his head about, shaking his worn-out face and displaying his stained teeth: an old dog who didn't want to give up. And looking back, I caught a glimpse of a golden retriever who was just lying there with his face pressed down on his paws, motionless, lost in despair.

This was my first visit to an animal pound, and not even in my imagination had I pictured what it would be like. I had simply not been interested. Now these poor creatures were showing me an aspect of life that I had never considered. My mind seemed to be linked to some strange input and I couldn't just brush aside what was now unfolding in front of me. I looked around and saw the staff taking the dogs for a walk or giving them food, and I observed how decently they handled the animals, even though they were abandoned and might only be able to live for another few days. Without talking to them, I could sense their respect for living things. The fact that they had chosen to work for the RSPCA itself suggested their special feeling for animals.

My mind turned to the concepts of mercy and compassion, something I'd only previously ascribed to humans, never thinking it appropriate between humans and animals. After all, it had been common in Hong Kong for us to see the chicken or fish we'd selected at the market killed in front of us to ensure its freshness. Then I remembered how Ka-ching, when only a small child, had been troubled for quite a while after she'd been to one of those markets, although I kept assuring her that this was a very normal Chinese practice. Could one become inured to cruelty, learn to be indifferent to suffering? But what was required to be compassionate towards animals? Perhaps a love for life itself, or did it require a bigger heart, a less selfish attitude, a deeper understanding of the world and the creatures that inhabit it? At this moment I felt challenged and became undecided.

Then I heard my husband and my daughter's voices: 'This dog is it! He's the one! He's what we'd like to have!' They were standing in front of the dog and calling him by various typical German male dog names.

'Hi, Fritz, good boy,' Ka-ching said. The dog raised his ears and stood up. My husband, Adalbert, started to talk in German: '*Ja, mein Suesser!*'

This was really like love at first sight. It could change fate. Would I be able to hold out against it?

'What sort of dog is he? I've never seen such a dog before.' I wanted to alert my family to the need for further consideration. I should at least try, if only to be fair to myself.

'He's obviously a mix,' Adalbert replied. 'Probably half German shepherd. Look how handsome he is. Mixed dogs are much better.' Then he bent down to greet him. 'Hello, Max.' I remembered my husband and I had talked about names for a son when I was pregnant, and he told me he wanted his son to be called Max.

The dog moved his head sideways, a bit puzzled, stepped forward and jumped up against the fence, lolling out his big tongue. This was more than just a smile—he seemed to be laughing. Later we found out that his name really was Max. No wonder he was so stirred up.

I was desperately trying to find a rational response: 'We'd better look carefully before we make a decision. We're not simply buying a toy to play with for one or two years, this will be a long-term companion. We'll be living with him and taking care of him for the rest of his life. It's better not to rush into any commitments.'

I knew this was not the right time to be giving lectures,

that I should have made this speech before we'd started the trip, but I also knew that it was probably my last chance to exercise my discretion as a potential dog owner, my right to say 'no'.

Almost immediately my husband replied: 'You have to trust me, I know these creatures very well and he's really very special, the best we could find.'

My husband did know a lot about dogs. He'd grown up with them, and although my daughter's knowledge was only superficial I fully understood that I was the least qualified to accept or reject any of the dogs here, let alone this remarkable creature.

'Let's wait for a few more months, then we can see more of them before choosing one. We've just landed in Sydney and we haven't even had time to breathe properly yet.'

But Ka-ching insisted: 'Why wait? He's the best. There'll be no second chance, we must take him today!'

Now I started to feel nervous. Turning my head to face the dog I showed him a 'not welcome' look, but he seemed unconcerned. Seeing him so much at ease even at this very moment of his destiny I couldn't utter another word, although my mind was still searching for reasons to refuse him. First, despite his good looks he'd been abandoned, so he must have been unmanageable, and he was not a pure breed, so he might have strange character traits and be difficult to train. Whatever the reason, I was not prepared to accept him. Yet I couldn't seem to shake the defeated feeling that surrounded me. Indeed, life is very often not what we expect.

In order to let us see the dog more clearly he was taken out of the cage, and as soon as he was freed he twirled around us in ecstasy and then raised his left leg against my husband's jeans and peed. Was this a demonstration to the other dogs that he had found his luck or had he simply claimed a potential master by leaving his mark on Adalbert's leg? What sort of dog was this?

'No problem, it's just an accident.' Surprisingly Adalbert, normally so obsessive about cleanliness, didn't mind at all, and as the staff apologised, this dog's good fortune seemed abundant.

Ka-ching was jumping around and yelling: 'Wow! This time you and Dad have been really efficient. We've found our dog at our first attempt. Sydney must be our lucky land, don't you think so, Mum?'

I didn't know what to say, except: 'Well in that case, you'll have a new best friend. He'll be like a little brother.'

'No, not a little brother, he'll be my big brother. I've read that a dog's one year equals a human's seven years!'

I saw her sudden surge of pride. But if that was really the case, then this dog was already a teenager, with a teenager's rebelliousness, selfishness, unsteady moods and destructive tendencies. He might actually be dangerous . . .

'Oh, Mum, why don't you say something? Just look at how cute he is! Now my dream has really come true.'

I rather thought it was the dog's dream that was coming true. He'd already been at the shelter for six days and if he was still not claimed by the following day he would have to be put him down in accordance with the regulations. This certainly put a lot of pressure on me, for it was clear that my refusal would mean a death sentence for him. Which would win, my mind or my heart—either a rational choice to reject him because of my own vulnerable situation or a surrender due to the kindness of my heart? It seemed incredible that such a good-looking dog had not been claimed right away, that he'd had to wait until almost the last day to meet his luck. I imagined I could hear the Bell of Doom ringing and see him being led down the path to the Gate of Death. While I hated being forced into taking him, I discovered that day that I did feel compassion towards this poor dog.

I looked at the other ten or more barking dogs as they moved restlessly backwards and forwards. They all shared the same look of anguish as their eyes called out, *Help, Help*. I turned my head away and saw our dog dancing around my husband, wagging his big bushy tail, expressing a newfound pleasure. 'Well, he's not at all a simple-minded one,' I told myself. Somehow I was charmed by his cheekiness; maybe his determination and that bit of confidence would be enough to win my heart. He turned his eyes towards me, telling me he was sure to win, and realising I was fighting an already lost battle against this newly risen current of emotion I smiled, if only to give him a good impression. Then I gazed at the other dogs again. It was impossible to save them all, but at least we could save this one. Perhaps, after all, he was destined to be our companion.

According to its rule of confidentiality, the RSPCA could not disclose the dog's background and under what circumstances he ended up as a 'stray', so we never discovered why he'd been abandoned or what his previous life had been like. All we were told was that he had just turned two and that he was part German shepherd, which was easily seen by the black patch on his body and the shape of his tail, but the other part was not so discernible. His colour and face resembled a dingo, and his size was just between the two. It seemed we needed to trust that it would all work out.

I examined him more closely: yes, this was indeed a unique creature. With his handsome face and his body covered with a thick, smooth orange-brownish coat that sparkled in the sun, his smart appearance was something no one could overlook. His extra-large ears moved constantly upwards and sideways to inspect his surroundings, his dark nose was long and showed a hint of arrogance, and most of the time his mouth was slightly open to show his happy nature, while at the same time giving you a glimpse of his sharp teeth. It was easy to imagine how he might look in a fight. He had an athletic figure, a slim body supported by four strong, compact legs. His eyelashes were long for a dog and the dark brown eye markings made his eyes stand out. They spoke to me, and somehow I knew that he understood a lot more than I could ever have imagined.

I put my hand on his head and stroked him gently, asking myself if I would want to spend the rest of his life with him. He was only two, so it was possible that we would be together for the next eleven or twelve years. Was I ready to start my new life and share happiness and sorrow with a four-legged being in a land I hardly knew?

It was the tenderness, like that of a lover, that finally captured me. It shone from those two wide and deep eyes. They seemed to say: 'Take me and I'll give you the love of your life.' What a charming, vibrant creature. How could I not be touched?

CHAPTER TWO

# THE DECISION

While we were still in Hong Kong and after we'd decided to emigrate to Sydney, Ka-ching had asked persistently for our agreement to adopt a dog, to protect our new home but mostly to be her pet and friend. Our Queen of Cats, Mimi, was already very old and ill, and although we'd made all the necessary arrangements for her to come with us, we were aware that she might leave us at any time, especially knowing that her stubborn determination would mean she'd die where she felt most comfortable. And so it was. She died in her Hong Kong home just one month before our move. One night, without much fuss, she said goodbye to us all and dragged her frail body to the back of the kitchen to die.

We were all saddened by Mimi's sudden departure, but it was Ka-ching who was most affected for she had lost her best companion. Soon her friends started saying their fare-wells to her and she became very emotional. We thought it would help to promise her a dog, so she would have some-thing to look forward to in Sydney. As soon as we landed she reminded us of our promise, and so it happened that 'looking for a dog' seemed to be on the top of our agenda. I hadn't expected, however, that within a month of our arrival in this new country I'd have to receive a new member into our family. This felt like a betrayal of our beloved Mimi, who had been with us for fourteen years.

I have always found the idea of adoption intriguing, because it means taking someone or something into your home with the intention of providing love and care for as long as required. For me, the essence of adoption is the renewal of life, the giving of a chance for a new start, expecting that the new life will be better than the old one. Yet while any decision to adopt should be grounded on the virtues of compassion and charity, it has been used as a means of compensating for some form of inadequacy or incompleteness, as in the case of the adoption of a child into a childless family.

While observing the other potential dog owners at the RSPCA kennels, I couldn't help questioning the purity of their decisions to adopt an animal and whether there was an underlying self-interest involved. Dogs are useful animals for guarding the home and their company can comfort the lonely heart, but discounting those positive values, how many would be ready to offer food and shelter without expecting some-thing in return?

Was this the case in our situation? Would our decision be more for the benefit of the dog or ourselves? It would certainly be an adoption with two purposes in mind: to enhance the security of our home and to give our daughter a companion. The dog might be deeply grateful but he could not know what was expected of him or why we wanted him, and most of all he would have no choice in the matter.

The vulnerable are at their weakest in adoption, because they surrender their lives to a stranger and an entirely uncer-tain future. As the person adopting, you feel there is an overwhelming power at work, the power to alter a destiny, and you are the powerful one. 'I would be empowered, I could change a life, his life,' I told myself. What I didn't know at that time was what magic this dog could perform and how that magic would change all our lives.

I turned to the staff and said: 'We need to think about it, can we give you a call tomorrow, to let you know what we've decided?'

'Of course, that's what people normally do,' I was told.

Yes, we definitely needed time to discuss it more fully, including committing everyone to sharing in the respon-sibility of taking care of our new friend. My husband and daughter must of course allow me time to reconsider. I didn't like events to fall in upon me, I always wanted to have control of my life. I felt that one more day might help to steer the course of my life back onto a safe track. They did not protest.

It was as if, for them, the outcome was already a foregone conclusion.

When we reached home I tried to forget the encounter and went about my normal housework. Ka-ching was quiet and stayed mostly in her room. I knew she was thoughtful, too. No one talked about what we were going to do regarding the dog—perhaps they didn't want to hear my 'no'.

At breakfast the next morning Adalbert asked: 'So, are we going to take him? We need to call the RSPCA. Today is supposed to be his last day.'

I stared out the window and said: 'I'm not sure.'

'But I'm certain he's exactly the right one, we couldn't find a better dog.' His voice was determined, and his face serious. Then I thought, I had given up my career and agreed to move to a totally new country, so I might as well agree to accept this dog. I heard myself saying: 'Well then, okay, we'll have him.'

And just like that it was done—we owned a dog before I knew what was happening. I wanted so much to say something more, but somehow the words stuck in my throat. Perhaps I was still exhausted from our move to Sydney; perhaps it was the piles of books, clothes, kitchen stuff and more still to be arranged; perhaps it was due to the loss of my career and the prospect of only being a housewife; perhaps I was dreading something I didn't yet know, something deep inside me. But you couldn't tell from my big brave smile.

My husband ran off to share the good news with my daughter, and within a few minutes they came to inform me: 'It's all arranged. He'll have a desexing operation and all the necessary vaccinations this afternoon and we'll pick him up tomorrow morning.'

'Mum, today is such a wonderful day, and tomorrow he'll be ours!'

I saw her face glowing with elation, while I was telling myself that this was like a 'river of no return'. We were adding something into our lives that we could not give back, yet what was this something supposed to be? Strictly speaking, by persuading me to accept the dog my husband and daughter had altered the direction of my life path, and I had given in to the supposedly higher call of compassion. Was this negligence or was it done out of some deeper understanding?

At the moment of decision, how do we know we've made the right one, how can we foretell the future? I felt a current rising in front of me, but there was no way to avoid it now, I simply had to let it take me. Like the move to Sydney. I was uprooted and just floating along.

I remembered that time, back in Hong Kong, when my sister's plan to buy a dog had finally been cancelled despite the persistent urging of her children and after several trips to the pet shop. It was not that she was ungenerous, she was simply scared by the implication of caring for another species. Other people might say: 'Well, it's only keeping a dog, no big commitment', but I knew that my sister took caring for animals very seriously. I believe that she knew she would find it hard to balance her self-interest against the needs of a pet, and that she didn't want to risk later regretting letting her children have one.

That evening before going to bed I sat quietly in the family room and pictured how it would be with this dog lying down on the floor, sitting up barking and walking in and out of our home, how I would have to fit him into my schedule and let myself into his. A home with an animal. Sharing my life with a four-legged stranger.

I knew what we could do if the dog turned out to be unsuitable in some way: we could either give him away or simply abandon him back to the RSPCA. That's what a lot of people would do without a bad conscience, thinking it's only an animal, after all. But I understood what it meant for us to be adopting a new member into our family, what it meant for me to be the mother of a dog, and I also knew that there was no use talking about it. It never helped to talk about the challenges of life. It's never the right approach to imagine frustration at the very beginning. Instead of dwelling on possible negative outcomes, I told myself that it was going to be a rewarding experience with a happy ending, and I slept that night with mixed feelings.

The following day, without any further lingering on the pros and cons of our decision, I put my signature on the adoption paper. I was taken aback by the simplicity of the whole transaction and the immediate transformation of my role. I had stepped over to the other side and all of a sudden I was a dog owner and I became the mother of Four-Legs, Max. In that instant I sensed time standing still. I was framed in a snapshot, and the memory of that moment would never fade.

## CHAPTER THREE

# MAX COMES HOME

We picked up Max after he'd had the operation. He'd been put in a kennel in a large room with six or seven other dogs, all similarly caged, most likely for rest after surgery of some kind. He was lying down, obviously tired, although his eyes were wide open, and when he saw us he got up and started wagging his tail, gently but apprehensively. He recognised our faces, our scent, our eyes. There was no mistaking that our second arrival meant much more than just another visit, but he waited patiently, not showing any sign of excitement. He seemed to understand the importance of good behaviour at this moment, while at the same time trying not to agitate the other poor dogs. It was not what I'd expected, this composed and sophisticated manner, not a bark, not a stir, accepting his fate without dramatic movements. Yet this was his rescue, and the beginning of the end of misery.

He was let out of the cage and put on a leash for us to take him home. He stayed low and humble, a bit embarrassed, for his good fortune now was witnessed by all with whom he had earlier shared an uncertain future. He looked straight ahead, his eyes loaded with emotion, and walked quietly, almost apologetically, out of the room. I could see the determination in his face, his tightly closed mouth showing a serious attitude, as if he had made the decision to leave. It was a solemn moment, until suddenly the room was roaring with deafening howls and barks. It was like the other dogs were saying goodbye to him, wishing him good luck, or perhaps they were protesting and complaining. I found it quite amusing as it was reminiscent of a climax of an orchestral piece, but my daughter was startled and covered her ears. I had never imagined such a scene, and for the first time in my life I had to reconsider what dogs were capable of. We humans couldn't comprehend what those sounds meant, we could only guess. Did the dogs know what was going on? Could they know that being led away by a human meant something promising? Yet here they were, totally helpless to life's dealings, without a choice. I caught sight of the kelpie in the middle of the room: he was fiercely yelling, 'No, it's not fair, it's not fair.' It would never be fair.

I was moved by the defencelessness of these abandoned dogs, passively subject to whatever of life's chances came their way through the humans who controlled their world. This was innocence in its purest form, pleading for a chance or simply hoping for life, yet it was impossible for them to realise what that meant and how it could be achieved. Whereas humans could always manage their own existence to some extent or other, and even, in extreme circumstances such as war, famine or natural disaster, they could fight, beg or cheat in order to help themselves, these animals could not even talk about it. And it was this that gave their innocence so pitiable a quality.

Max didn't turn his head to take a last look. Perhaps he didn't want to risk any chance of a return, as though by merely looking back we might change our minds; we might—I might. I was still not totally convinced. Or was it too unbearable for him to see his former companions still suffering? I fixed my eyes on him, wanting to find out more before he was completely ours. He quickened his pace just before leaving the room and took the lead, and in those last few steps I saw him cross over the boundary from one extreme to another, from a near end to a promising start. It was a moving personal drama.

As the Gate of Death closed behind him the ringing stopped and the door on the other side, the Door of Rebirth, opened. He took a big stride, and in the last second a long jump. He had made it, and as soon as we were outside the building he celebrated. His eyes were bright with jubilation and his tired body was now full of vitality. I noticed his triumphant nose and victorious smile as he led the way to his renewed existence. He had won, and he had won my heart. We stared at each other, overwhelmed by what it had taken to get us to this moment.

It was the ninth day of September 1999—numerically, 9.9.1999. I would never forget this date. In Chinese the number 9 sounds exactly the same as the sound of the character for dog. This was indeed an interesting coincidence. What I didn't know that day was how this would mark out the rest of my life.

A few moments later we were heading home, accompanied by four more legs. It was a clear spring morning with a blue cloudless sky and a light breeze that brought flower-scented fresh air into the car, so the hour-long drive was very pleasant. The green parks with their beautiful big trees were a wonderful sight for us new arrivals, as it was a totally different environment from Hong Kong and we still didn't quite know how to handle the unexpected delight. A month before we'd been ensnared in pollution with our views blocked by high-rise buildings; here we felt almost incapable of fully appreciating the beauty around us. The warm spring sun had awakened the land, and its different plants and creatures were now competing in the surge towards new life. Nature's rhythms were at work, and everywhere something was trying to establish its existence.

I was sitting in the back, allowing our daughter to have a good time with her father; these two were now sharing their excitement in welcoming their new companion. They sang one song after another, bursting into laughter as they twisted the lyrics into jokes. I listened numbly, for I had to keep an eye on the two paws resting on the back seat just inches away from my neck. Max had been put into the very back of our four-wheel drive, where he had plenty of room to stretch himself or, if he wished, to have a nap, but for some reason he'd preferred to climb up and lean over the back of the rear seats. This position gave him the advantage of observing events taking place both in and outside the vehicle, but it also meant that I needed to be alert in order to oversee him. I wound down the window to let out the unpleasant smell emanating from his dusty coat and turned my head to look at him: this new beginning definitely required a thorough clean-up.

My mind started to work on how to organise my life with these extra four legs in it. Of course I should quickly finish reading the two books on dog training that I'd bought when we first made that promise to adopt a dog, but the more urgent question of setting up boundaries had to be addressed right away. Should we hire a professional trainer or send Max to a training school? Could a two-year-old still be trained? My husband wanted to speak German to him whereas I would probably just talk to him in English. Would he be confused or would he be like my daughter, who could master three languages? I shouldn't have high hope, and in any case what could I expect when I didn't even know what dogs knew about humans? Yes, the Chinese used to eat dogs (a few may continue to do so), and even nowadays to most Chinese dogs are just dogs. And this was only a beast with some ability to understand what was going on in his world, with excellent hearing and a nose that could distinguish many more scents than humans. I reflected when I'd disclosed my concern about living with a dog to a good friend in Hong Kong, how she'd looked at me in amazement and said: 'Well, it's only a dog, why are you so serious about it?' She was right, of course, we humans *shouldn't* be troubled by mere animals. But still I wondered if I would ever really be in complete control of this strange being and my new life with him in it.

I gazed at his blissful face, now at ease and full of confidence. What a dramatic escape from his misfortune, and what a drastically different world he was now in. There was a definite thrill of new possibilities and discoveries as his head kept busily moving from side to side, overwhelmed by the moving scenes outside: a cattle dog barking outside a butcher's shop, a cat dashing across the road, pigeons being fed by children, people laughing, flowers opening . . . moments of life in action, real and enticing. Stories of life passing, happy or sad, real or unreal, here a joke, there a whine. A gust of wind brushed by and fluffed his fur coat, sending several hairs flying in the air. Some landed on the seat and one settled on my shoulder. Inside the car, life was manifesting itself, too, as his eyes shone and his ears lengthened. Expression of joy. Arresting beauty. But I was in no mood for appreciating beauty.

My thoughts led me away from the scenes before me, and I found myself caught in an unexpected spiral where good sense didn't help. The prospect of dealing with an animal I didn't understand scared me: how could I manage to live with him in peace when I still wasn't sure how I would adjust to my own new life in Sydney? I didn't have enough confidence in myself, and how could I develop confidence while taking care of him? I was born and grew up in Hong Kong, in a Chinese community I knew very well. It had never been my dream to move away from my familiar community and be confronted with these uncertainties, and I had hesitated before embarking on this life-changing journey. It was for the sake of my family that I'd agreed to leave Hong Kong, and although some might have considered it courageous of me, I knew when I left what a huge load of apprehension I was carrying. The moment I first stepped onto Australian soil I realised how much I was going to miss my family, my friends and my work, and now I was faced with the task of educating this four-legged creature. The challenge of adjusting to my new world was something I'd prepared myself for, but adjusting to a dog before I'd properly settled in? In Hong Kong I'd taught Sociology at the university and I was confident enough in dealing with human affairs, but with dogs I'd had no experience at all. My heart started to sink and I seemed to be aching inside: I could see the way ahead, long and winding, its direction blurred by my insecurity.

I thought, too, of my husband's forthcoming two-month-long business trip to Hong Kong and Europe and my daughter's new school life the following month. I would then have to rely on myself, and only myself, to help her switch from the German way of learning to the new, highly competitive Australian education system. I still had to obtain an Australian driver's licence and then study street maps so I could find my way around, and I had no relatives who I could turn to for advice or assistance. We were used to having helpers at home in Hong Kong: the live-in maid who did the shopping and cooking, and the chauffeur who took care of the cars and drove us around. I really felt that I needed to worry about myself, to deal with my own self-esteem, before I could do anything for a pet, a task I certainly hadn't expected to be undertaking so soon. Besides, I had no idea what this might entail, other than the basic need of walking the dog. By taking Max on board, had I actually reduced myself to the mundane role of dog walker? When would I now find the time to enjoy my new life? As the words of my friend surfaced again in my mind, it occurred to me that this would surely be no 'peaceful, retired life'.

I remembered a story I'd read about an owner being bitten by her own dog as I edged further away from Max who, excited at the sight of some dogs running around in a park, was now trying to clamber over onto my side of the seat. He was obviously carried away by this adventurous trip and as yet had no understanding of the basic etiquette expected of him in our family. I was about to discharge my duty as his mistress and instruct him to calm down when he brushed his big fat tongue on my cheek. It was meant to be a quick kiss, out of overflowing emotion, I supposed, but I felt very dirty with that foul smell now on my cheek. I quickly searched for the pack of anti-bacterial wipes in my handbag to clean my face. I did not need a kiss from a dirty dog, a strange, abandoned four-legged animal. I put on my most horrible face and stared down at him but he seemed to misinterpret my expression and moved further towards me. Now half of his body was over on my side, and as he tried to put his head on my shoulder, drops of his saliva fell on my neck . . .

The car almost came to a sudden halt when I screamed. My husband looked in the rearview mirror and my daughter turned around in her seat, then after a few seconds they both began to laugh. 'The Chinese don't understand dogs,' I heard my husband say, as I frantically searched for ways to restore my dignity.

Confucianism places the most importance on rules and rites according to positions held in a structured environment. A newcomer no doubt disrupts this established order and, as a result, confusion will reign. It is in a state of confusion that one lacks wisdom and makes mistakes, the status quo is broken and harmony is destroyed. I was determined that this was not going to happen to us: we Chinese know how to prevent disaster and prepare ourselves for anything that might happen. I must set up new rules and rites, especially to keep the newcomer under control, before regret had a chance to make its presence felt. I must establish my authority in the house, especially after my husband leaves on his business trip. I would need the cooperation of my daughter; this would be decisive in the maintenance of our balance of power at home. I knew very well that happiness or unhappiness in our new life depended on this, and on how Max would perceive his new home and what he actually was—and this I still had to find out.

I thought of our life here: the private school my daughter would soon be starting, the Australian accent that was still a problem, the multicultural social fabric that I could never have imagined from my life in Hong Kong and, of course, the new friends we were all hoping to make.

I thought of my own life, without a job or a career, the life of a housewife, of shopping, washing, cooking, driving—and now, of course, walking and caring for Four-Legs. Suddenly I started missing my teaching jobs in Hong Kong, with those adult students whose limitless thirst for knowledge was the driving force for my hard work, and who in return gave me the awareness of myself as an intellectual, an entity other than a wife, mother and homemaker. I searched my mind for those ambitions I used to boast of and my early dreams of achieving something bigger than cooking good meals, raising children and managing a home. Something deeper in meaning, more demanding, sophisticated and refined, a more satisfying, ful-filling life, so to speak. But with the resignation from my job, emigration to Sydney, separation from my parents, siblings and supportive friends, and now the adopting of Max, I seemed to have given up everything I used to desire and taken up some-thing I wasn't quite happy to do . . . I wondered if I would be able to cope. I realised that I hadn't done nearly enough research before deciding to emigrate here, hadn't equipped myself properly for the unfamiliar and unexpected. I'd taken for granted that it would not be difficult, been naive to think that all would go smoothly. Now it was as if I found myself in a descending lift, aware that I was going down and unable to stop it, trying to hold on to something, at best a noble convic-tion, but weakened by self-doubt, being taken somewhere I didn't really want to go . . .

Max had now disappeared behind me, so I turned around and looked into the back of the car. He was curled up on the floor with his eyes half closed, breathing heavily. Finally he could relax, exhausted by the past week's events and the many expectations and disappointments, reassured at last that he had been accepted into a new family. Now he surely knew that a little rest wouldn't change his good luck. There was a long moment of silence: no more songs, no more jokes. We were back to reality after the thrill of the fresh start.

We passed one park after another, then the big mansions and the interesting terrace houses. The wind brought in the typical spring perfume of Sydney, the sun had softened a little and a patch of white clouds now hung in the sky. We were closer to home, a home that I still had to get used to. And the city itself: as well as its geography, I still had to find out what it offered other than the beauty of the harbour and its ocean beaches.

'Mum, do you think he will love our home?'

'I am certain he will. Besides, he has no choice, has he?'

'Yes, he has to love his home! I think he knows he's very lucky. Do you think he understands that, Dad?'

'Don't think they are stupid. Dogs know a lot. Look at his eyes, they tell you he's thankful.'

My husband was looking into the mirror once more. Max was up again, resting his paws on the back of the seat, fulfilled. I was quite entranced, unable to take my eyes off him, his zest and his joy.

I was again absorbed in my deep thoughts when I heard Ka-ching shout, 'Mum, come on, get out, we're home!'

I had not been conscious that the boot of the car had been opened, and I looked: he was there, with his eyes wide open, his nose stretched, his ears extended and his paws planted firmly on the driveway in front of the garage. His head kept moving to check his surroundings and he started pacing right and left, all prepared and ready for action. I was struck dumb by the bustling image he made and stunned by how fast life had changed. This 'other' being had entered onto the stage of our life, yet I hadn't even had the script ready.

Max had arrived home.

Home, where you could be your real self, Four-Legs, never mind a bit of misbehaviour or indiscretion, where you belonged and were accepted, a place of discovery where you could find out who you were, a destination after a journey and a resting place after an adventure. Surely Max knew all this, but right now home was a new excitement, for what it promised.

He turned himself swiftly around, investigating his new home with a few cursory sniffs here and there, practising the ritual of moving in. The bushy tail elevated a bit, brushing away the dust on the garage wall. He raised his leg against the small tree in front of the garage to mark his arrival before climbing up the stairs to the main gate. Then, perhaps realising that he should first have received permission from his new masters, he ran back down the stairs and sat down in front of us with his front paws placed neatly together, waiting for instructions. A first show of his obedience, as if to say: 'What now? What am I supposed to do now?' His gaze was fixed firmly on my husband, smartly recognising who was the real boss.

CHAPTER FOUR

# THE
# FIRST DAY

A spring morning with hairs in the air, drifting, swirling; golden, soft hairs; see them fly, see them making a spell. The movement of life, the scent of a materialised dream. Surely there would be a lot of vacuuming to do; suck them in and bury them—or would I catch them and collect them to make a reminiscence of our life together?

'*Suesser*, it's time for a thorough wash. Our home is a very clean place, you can't belong here with this terrible stink! It's no big deal, just a wash, you'll feel better afterwards. Now come to Dad . . . Good boy!'

I saw my husband bending down to talk to Max, as though he were a child. No, not a child, there was something more, something new and different in this kind of conversation. It was different to talking with our cat Mimi.

It had always seemed to me that cats, being superior animals—or so they believed—did not particularly enjoy having conversations with humans. Not that they were not loving, they just preferred their own way of expressing feelings. Our Mimi didn't follow commands, she would never come when called and she would jump onto our newspapers or whatever we were reading whenever she felt so inclined. Then, unexpectedly, when she turned fifteen, as if old age had brought a new understanding, she became almost cooperative. Even then our talk with her was limited to a few words of command, praise or games. I couldn't recall actually talking to her, but I remembered my daughter's letter urging her to be brave and explaining how important it was for her to take her medicine. That was when Mimi was very sick and she was being taken to the vet, just a year before she passed away. My daughter didn't ever talk to Mimi about this, as if she felt that a letter would somehow be more useful. It was strange how we dealt with creatures not of our kind, but how could we not talk to this dog, who was so expressive and eager to communicate?

My daughter was already busy taking out the hose and the shampoo. And I thought I'd never seen her feel so important. I remained standing at the corner watching her and Max: somehow I didn't want to participate. I had been forced into this situation, and as far as the plot to this point was concerned I felt I was still an outsider. I knew that after the wash I would have to become a full participant, so for now I was quite happy to be an observer.

Water now became an interesting medium: it ran out of the hose onto Max's thick fur, soaking through to his skin as the shampoo formed a lather that covered his body. The water was transforming his status—dissolving the old and bringing in the new. It was like a baptism, although this was rather an amusing image. Not a word was spoken. I could hear the sound of the water flowing on the ground as my husband and my daughter worked with great seriousness to clean Max: my husband using his hand to rub Max's body and tail and my daughter gently wiping his head and face with a small cloth.

It was clear that Max didn't enjoy the procedure, but he had attempted no resistance and now, all wet and skinny, he lay down in surrender, totally submissive and rather pitiable. He was thoroughly washed, not only his body but his mind and heart, and perhaps his miserable past as well: going down with the water that was now draining away. This was how a fresh start should begin, getting rid of the old, the dirt, the odour, the horror and the sorrow, to be renewed, refreshed, redeemed.

'Hey, Mum, why are you standing there? Can't you see he's shivering from the cold? Quick, pass me a towel!'

I brought a towel as quickly as I could and wrapped it around him, embracing him, touching him, stroking his wet hair. I wanted to cry, for this beginning, for the courage to start afresh, to take on the uncertainties and submit to life's possibilities. I held him tight and he looked deep into my eyes.

There was no cheekiness, no fooling around, it was trust between us now. I realised I was holding not just a new relationship but also a responsibility and a commitment. There was no going back, now I had to become involved, not just a little but fully, wholeheartedly, for him, for myself, for my family. I had to put courage into action, and an action that could be seen. That action had now started and life was marching on. It was the only way to win.

'Fine, my dear boy—welcome to our family. You be a good boy and I'll be your mum.'

He stood up, shook off the water. Drops splashed onto my face and clothes. I knew I had to get used to this, there would no longer be a clear separation between the human and the animal. I was going to have his hair on my body, too, but I hoped not the smell.

Leading the way, my daughter walked him up to his place in the family room next to the open kitchen. There we put the basket we'd bought from the RSPCA, filled it with a few pillows and covered them with a blanket: his bed. But his curiosity had turned on again and he was busy exploring things—the kitchen cabinets, the dining table, the chairs. And then he jumped onto the couch . . .

'Hey, get down, that's not your place.' My husband had raised his voice: the first lesson. He jumped off right away, a bit puzzled. My daughter took hold of his collar and brought him to his bed: 'Here is where you will lie. This is your place, do you understand?'

Max climbed onto his bed and gave a loud sigh, as if to puff out all that was depressing from the past week. I had never heard of a dog sighing like this, and I still haven't met a dog who could act so dramatically. It was a very human gesture. Observing him, I felt a strange insecurity slowly climbing up to my throat again. Was it due to my own changed identity? Or did I sense a certain unforeseeable challenge?

The first-day program planned by his thoughtful masters included a lavish lunch of beef and rice, followed by a tour of the house and an introduction to the boundary points and forbidden areas. Then he was driven to the nearest park, so that a healthy routine would be established right away. Here he met with neighbours of his kind and, of course, found his favourite spots to do his business. The evening arrived quietly and in a courteous manner, so as not to cause further concern. After dinner Max climbed into his bed, this time happily claiming possession of it, and arranged himself in the most comfortable position.

Darkness spread to cover every corner, and it finally landed on Max. His big brown eyes were hidden under his long eyelashes, his face rested on his paws and his tail was placed neatly next to his right leg. He was quite at ease, yet I knew he wasn't asleep—no, he couldn't be so relaxed so soon. I guessed he would get up and inspect everything again once I'd left the kitchen, but I rather wanted to stay for a while.

I stood in front of the glass door and looked out to the sky, then lowered my gaze to the dark swelling harbour. I thought of Hong Kong, of my mother there, now having dinner, and of the many people still shopping in the mall at this time of the evening. What a different world it was here, and what a different life I had started. I thought of the dogs there, too, not so many of them. They must be in the streets as well, or at least in the arms of their masters, cute little things that were carried around like babies. You didn't see them running in a park.

Once in Hong Kong I'd seen two dogs lying on a table in the middle of a very busy street to publicise 'animal rights'. There were posters and documents of various kinds and the person in charge explained how her group tried its best to take care of abandoned dogs. They were supposed to be nice people rescuing dogs, but even then I'd wondered why they were not able to feel for those two poor creatures, probably drugged in order to be lying so still in the midst of all that traffic and people. I can still remember how they looked. With no spirit in their eyes, it was as though they'd already given up hope and just accepted their fate. I was surprised that I'd still kept that picture in my mind.

Then I thought of Julie, a little abandoned Japanese dog. I remembered how my oldest sister brought her home when I was about thirteen years old. Despite my mother's reluctance to accept her, Julie stayed with us for three months. This was my first experience with an animal, but Julie wasn't able to generate any loving feelings in me. I was quite a confused teenager, and this extra member in the family only brought more noise and chaos into our home. It also meant that we had less to eat. My siblings and I quietly complained when we saw food being given to the dog. Life in Hong Kong was difficult at the time and many families, including my own, were trying really hard to make ends meet.

Julie was a restless dog who barked a lot, and we simply couldn't understand what she wanted. She became so ill that we had to take her to the vet, and in the taxi she nervously vomited on my father's lap. I was surprised how gentle he was with her. My father was a temperamental person, yet it seemed that this poor sick little dog was able to draw out the soft part of him. At the time I'd wondered how this was possible, and of course I would never have believed that a dog would one day affect me in the same way.

After that trip to the vet Julie's life changed and the reason was clear: we were simply not able to cope. My mother asked: 'How can we manage, when we can't even manage all these kids?' Indeed, there were already six of us at home for her to feed, and every time she gave Julie food I could see she wasn't happy, although she would never have let Julie starve. Like most Chinese people at that time, she had hardly any feelings for animals, and I found it illogical that she hadn't rejected Julie in the first place. We all knew that if Julie hadn't been so sick my parents might have kept her, but in the end a relative from the country came to fetch her. My father believed that life in the countryside would suit her better. I was quite relieved that the dog was finally going, but my father seemed to be sad, and just before Julie was taken away I saw him gently stroke her, a tenderness I had never seen in him before.

I quickly forgot this first encounter and grew up with little feeling for animals. They could be cute and cuddly, but they were of little significance, except for functional purposes and for food. It was probably pleasant to touch them and stroke their soft fur, but you certainly didn't give them your heart. My life then was too busy to be bothered with unnecessary sentiment, there were more important things to deal with, so why spend precious time with a dog with whom I couldn't even communicate? I had learned not to misplace my feelings.

Later, when I married, I had to accept my husband's cat unconditionally, for she was there before I moved in. Of course I soon became used to living with Mimi, but she and I led different lives. It was not my role to take care of her and she never needed anything from me until her very old age. She and my husband had an excellent connection, so for many years she was almost oblivious of my existence. My husband was her real love and my daughter, first as a baby and later as a child, never ceased to amuse her. I was merely the one who brought home her food and cleaned her litter box. There was no necessity to cross the boundary to construct a relationship with this animal.

To be honest, I had always found the extravagant sentiments expressed by animal lovers somewhat embarrassing, especially the way they treated their dogs and cats as almost human and granted them the same, if not more, love and care than other members of their family. I had told myself that I would always guard against this kind of stupidity.

I quietly opened the door and walked into the garden to let out what I had been suppressing and was delighted to take in some fresh and invigorating night air. Outside I could hear the gentle sound of the waves lapping along the foreshore and see the Harbour Bridge hanging proudly above the dark mass of glittering water in moon light, a symbol of high hopes and fantasies. It was as if we all needed to climb up to somewhere and be euphoric at least for a while. But then after being at the top and having a great view, must we not also climb down to the mundane life? Humans all desire to achieve more and to live better, even though we don't quite know what we actually want. We had moved, and we had accomplished what we'd planned some years ago. So far everything had gone according to our plans. Even getting a dog had been easy. 'Are we satisfied and happy now?' I asked myself.

My husband and my daughter had gone to bed, and I wondered what had been in their minds before they fell asleep. Were they at all apprehensive about our new start, as I was? Would my daughter be happier in her new life now that she had a dog? From the way she'd behaved today, it had certainly given her a sense of importance. And what did my husband feel, now that he had fulfilled his ambition of living in one of the most beautiful cities in the world? It was not difficult to understand his pride in his achievement, for he had accomplished a lot in his life, from Germany to Hong Kong and now to Sydney. His staff in Hong Kong were already waiting for his instructions, and clients in Germany, whose trust he had successfully won, were anticipating his arrival three weeks later. By then I would be standing on my own.

The half-moon that hung above the trees seemed unusually close. It was telling me the history of mankind. Human beings had always fought for and defended what they thought was theirs, and amidst all their struggles they had often been baffled by their own survival, which rarely came without a great price. And as I pondered, the ancient stars looked down and found me, perhaps amused by my deep contemplation. On the opposite shore, the city skyline formed a frame for the reality of daily life and a struggle for existence into which so many people were locked. I had now come face to face with my own reality, and I must stretch out my arms to embrace it. This had been one day in my life and tomorrow would be a new day, starting with Max.

As I stepped back to the kitchen, he yawned. He was really sleepy. Perhaps he wouldn't want to find out anything more tonight, and perhaps I shouldn't continue searching my soul. I certainly shouldn't burden myself with any further self-discovery. Right now my head was like an electrical box with a number of wires, some connected and some entangled, all in desperate need of reorganisation. Perhaps I, too, should go to bed. What a day. What a change.

'Good night, Max. Sleep tight. It's all fine, you are part of our reality now.'

I heard his deep breathing, air taking in and pushing out. His eyes were like slits, watching me still. I touched his front paws where his face now rested, those little bones and long nails, and I ran my fingers along his back and felt his coat, skin, flesh and bone. This was clearly existence.

He had escaped the finality of the seventh day. He had just been at the Gate of Death, but God had lifted him up and turned him around to face me.

## Chapter Five

# ACCEPTANCE

A friend of mine once told me: 'You will be surprised what God has in store for you—not just a little surprise but big surprises.' I didn't know what she was talking about and I certainly didn't give any more thought to those 'big surprises'.

On the morning of 10 September 1999 I opened my eyes to a different world. I remember that it was bright and that the light breeze wafting in from the balcony stroked my face and cleansed my mind. I didn't know then that from this day onwards I would never again be the same person. If we think experience is just a way of learning, we underestimate the power of those experiences that not only change our thoughts and attitudes but actually close a door on our previous concerns and open another to reveal new dimensions in our lives. On that day, my heart was beating as though it expected something extraordinary to take place.

I looked at my husband, wondering whether he was just as excited, but he was very much at ease with the prospect of our new family set-up, confident of his own decision. After all, he'd grown up with family dogs. As for my daughter, she was too young to understand the implications of what we had done: to her, a dog was simply a playmate who would give her plenty of fun. I realised that I was the one who would feel the real impact, and to my surprise, I suddenly felt ready for this reorganisation of our domestic life: physically strong enough and mentally and emotionally prepared for it.

I tiptoed quietly into the kitchen trying not to wake Max, but he was already sitting at the entrance to the kitchen and he greeted me with his big sharp white teeth, totally relaxed and thoroughly at home. Perhaps he was thinking of his morning exercise and wondering what delicious food I had bought for him. Max had required only a little time to understand the drastic change in his life: after all, adaptation to new circumstances may be more a matter of the heart than of the mind. Animals, unlike humans, don't wait to analyse new situations. Was this a survival instinct, to accept something rather than not?

He looked me in the eye, softening his features. This was a face for his mistress, mother and owner. It told me he didn't own himself anymore, he now belonged, and was included as part of the family. I could clearly see the difference between hell and heaven, between being abandoned and being warmly welcomed into our home. I called my husband and daughter and announced the beginning of our new life.

Our first walk together was taken with enthusiasm and a lot of fun, but I also returned home with a few observations. I put away the English and Chinese novels I'd placed in the family room a few days earlier, and replaced them with books on dogs. Of course, I was hoping that my family would be immensely interested in perfecting their knowledge and skills in handling Max. But I wasn't fooled. I could guess what it would be like in the coming months and years. I would be the one who'd have to organise both myself and the dog, yet I would not give up reminding the other members of my family of the importance of our task.

I started our breakfast with a quote from Dr Patricia McConnell's book, *The Other End of the Leash*:

> *Dogs don't come speaking [a language], and they don't come reading your mind. If your dog doesn't listen to your commands, it well might be because he is confused.*

I said the word 'confused' twice and looked at Max, who was listening with a frown.

> *Happy, well-trained dogs understand a wealth of information from the sounds that their humans make . . . but if you analyze our behaviour carefully, sometimes I think it's a miracle that our dogs understand us at all.*

I had a quick check on our dog: he lifted up his face and winked at me.

'A miracle! You know, we are dealing with a miracle here. Or, actually, we have to accomplish a miracle. Do you understand what I'm talking about?' I asked my daughter.

She looked at me for a second and shook her head: 'Dad, you grew up with dogs, you should answer Mum's question.'

'But they know a lot and are remarkably smart. Just be consistent,' was his casual response, as he turned to the financial pages of his newspaper.

I continued to lecture on our responsibilities as dog owners, and my daughter became more and more excited about her new role, assuring me of her readiness to teach and lead Max. I knew I couldn't ask much from my husband; he'd probably already started thinking about his forthcoming trip. It was as though he'd been responsible only for setting it all up—and I couldn't say he hadn't done a great job—but he was looking so relaxed that I knew the ball was now firmly in my court.

'Isn't it true that almost every household in this city has a dog?' my daughter sighed. 'Are they all this serious about it?'

I didn't answer, but I couldn't help asking the same question.

Three weeks later I said goodbye to my husband at the airport, and as he was about to walk towards the restricted area he turned to me and asked: 'Will you be fine with him?'

I nodded, and gave him a brave smile.

I quickly established a routine of rising early and taking Max out for his morning walk, while my daughter prepared for her school day. Then came the rain, which turned some parts of the park into mud. I was able to stop Max from drinking out of the puddles, but I couldn't prevent him from running in the mud. After battling against the wind and rain—which Max doubtless thought was great fun—on our arrival home my agile dog leapt straight out of the car and dashed down to the kitchen to his breakfast. I followed, exhausted, to find a trail of mud and other bits and pieces from the park on the carpet of our newly renovated home. Although I gave Max a lecture on hygiene and cleanliness, I could see that I would have to wipe him down every time we came back from our walks. I then bought a bucket and some small towels and resolved that from now on I would do this twice a day: easier to clean my dog than my home.

I soon found that my jogging shoes were wearing out from walking on damp grass and my toes were icy cold. That early spring was especially chilly for me, so I bought rubber boots, several pairs of thick socks and a sturdy raincoat, took out my thick scarf and new thermal underwear, and the following day off we went to the park, now properly equipped. And when the strong sun returned I went to the market and bought big hats and loads of sunscreen, remembering how my mother had warned me about skin cancer. I also realised that my former habit of wearing make-up whenever I went out was no longer necessary: not only because Max wouldn't appreciate it, but I would also have looked rather out of place among the dog walkers and their dogs. What was more important were the little plastic poo bags that I'd never heard of. I found them everywhere: in the park, at the corner store and at the vet's, and I never forgot to carry a few in my waist bag whenever we went out.

So, armed with apprehensive determination and stubborn persistence, I started my role as dog owner. I now felt fully prepared to raise my four-legged boy. 'No matter what, off we'll go, every day,' I told myself.

One day, I was awoken by a strong, foul smell of some kind coming from outside my room. I got up and followed my nose to the kitchen, where I found Max curled up in his bed with wide-open eyes. From his reserved manner—no wagging tail, no getting up to greet me with his signature smile—I knew he was trying to tell me something. He remained in his bed, fully alert, with tall ears and a tightly closed mouth, but those worried eyes were still checking on my response. I was puzzled, and pulled by my nose I went downstairs where, just at the entrance hallway, I found his droppings: bits, pieces and mashes, spreading around to form a big mess. I stood there, horrified. 'Oh, my God!' was all I could say.

A week later it happened again, and again the following week. It took a few of these incidents for me to accept that this was part of the deal of the adoption, that Max had probably been born with a sensitive stomach or had acquired an allergy, and what would be would be. If diarrhoea was part of him, then I must accept the fact that I would now have to spend an hour or so cleaning up his mess whenever it happened— and perhaps frequently. Would this take away my determination to be a loving mistress or would it constitute an obstacle? Should I be prepared to spend my valuable life dealing with a dog's diarrhoea? Wouldn't anyone call this a challenge, of the most demeaning kind?

I couldn't help feeling a bit cheated and I desperately needed to find a good and valid reason to justify my situation. I'd farewelled my family, friends and work, left my familiar Chinese community and intellectual environment behind, perhaps for good, and in doing so I'd moved away from the satisfaction and comfort they would offer me. Had I made all these compromises and come to a new land only to become the servant of an animal? My mind was full of questions that made me search my soul for the purpose of my life. As I knelt there cleaning up the mess, I suddenly realised what it really meant to be starting from the beginning.

I knew that Max was deeply sorry and remorseful for the trouble he caused: each time he saw me working hard to clean up after his accidents he would sit by me to give me emotional support. He would watch my long and frustrated face with deep contrition and sincere sympathy, knowing how much I hated doing this job that I now must do, grateful that I did not punish him but kindly accepted his weakness.

And so life moved on, with hardly time for a pause. I was kept busy assisting my daughter with her new school and extracurricular activities, while I rushed around establishing our new life in Australia. And then there was Max. Before my husband reappeared, we had already developed a special relationship.

# THE NEW
# LIFE

## Chapter Six

# THE WORLD OF FOUR-LEGS

If you consider your dog as a family member and not just a pet to play with or a guard dog to watch your home, you must first find out about his character, likes and dislikes, strengths and weaknesses. In other words, you must get to know him, and the best way to do that is to be in his world. Animals do not desire our world, they would much rather simply sit and observe us and the events that revolve around us. In the beginning, I'd had to make a big leap over to Max's side in order to experience what it was like to be non-human. The challenge lies in how high you set your standards and what results you set out to achieve.

You can keep a dog without ever trying to understand what's going on in his brain or heart. You can feed him, take him to the backyard at business times and occasionally give him a wash or take him for a walk—this is about all that is strictly necessary for keeping a pet at home—and you may then think you have fulfilled your responsibilities. But if you want to go beyond the strictly necessary and have a give-and-take relationship, a communication that is more than obeying commands or just living together, you must participate in the events of the animal's life and let him join in the family activities. For living a life does not mean only eating and sleeping, washing and walking.

The real trial is finding meaning and satisfaction in the repetitive daily routine of living with and taking care of your dog, and the most important aspects of this are consistency—in education, training, care and other activities—and patience—the ability to wait and see, to give all the time it takes to achieve an intended outcome, always allowing for the unexpected and the fact that the focus of your attention cannot speak and has very much a mind of his own. There is no consistency without patience. You have to learn respect for another species, discard the view that animals don't matter much, and acknowledge that they have the right of choice, whether to eat this or that food or to wear or not wear a jumper. The fact is that you are actually sharing a life together, and respecting each other's style and ways of behaving should be part of the deal.

In adoption, whether two-legged or four-legged, the most important yet most often unacknowledged requirement is love. If there is no love at the first encounter it is important that you somehow develop and exhibit a loving manner. It isn't always easy. Love is interactive, it goes both ways, so you must somehow learn to break down or cross over any barriers that may arise.

I rolled over with a heavy weight in my heart, then almost fell out of bed to enter the world of Max. Clarity caught me by surprise, softened me and gave me new meanings. I had, quite unexpectedly, found myself captivated and subdued as Max held me to my commitment simply by his gaze, his movements and his posture. Although he rarely asked for anything more than his daily routines of walking and playing with us, food to eat and a bed to sleep in, Max could always tell me what he wanted, and what he wanted most of all was my love.

In my relationship with Max, I knew I had to keep that loving feeling alive and well, for what could be the value of living in a world without love? For humans as well as animals. Love is the sustaining force to a satisfying life. I realised that by allowing myself to really love Max, I would actually be giving love to myself, and that by showing his unfailing love to me he would receive more love from me. This is how things work: how much we get from a relationship hinges on how much we give. It's when we no longer show feelings of love that life becomes boring and superficial. So I learned to be sensitive, generous and expressive whenever I was with Max.

Max's world was one of the senses: seeing, hearing, smelling. His eyesight was so good that he could see the smallest detail, and he possessed an acute sense of hearing. It was through interpreting these combined senses that we communicated. I had never before been so aware that I could guess at meanings

and draw conclusions through signs, images and represen-
tations. I often observed how he behaved according to the
different sounds he heard, sounds that told him he was safe
or warned him of danger. And what he smelt had the power to
overwhelm him: as he walked determinedly towards a smell
he was literally being led by his nose. I could hardly blame him
for not listening to my orders whenever he detected a truly
extraordinary scent.

Max's world of action was so contagious that I had to join
in his never-ending activity, simply playing along and reacting
to him. Walking, running, chasing, jumping, catching, behind
me, ahead of me, around the corner, under a tree, at the traffic
lights, across the park; I was dragged along, pushed forward,
pulled along, kick-started from the back. I didn't mind that
I was tired and would be surprised that I still had plenty of
energy. Never in my life had I performed so many movements, gestures and actions, and once I started I could not
stop. Because of Max's charm, I was drawn into a strange kind
of vitality, like being transported to a fairyland where the fun
would never end.

This was not a matter of intelligence or rationality, it was
a matter of dedication and participation in very simple acts.
Repetitive play was most anticipated and welcome during our
games, and the more these actions, signs and sounds were
repeated, the more acceptable they became as their meanings
became clearer. And that's how we grew together, my Four-
Legs and I.

There must have been times when Max probably found me

strange, even a bit silly, such as when I would just sit and watch him instead of attending to the television program or the book I was reading, or when I would lower myself to the floor and walk on all fours to come close to him. He was conscious of how intimately I observed the way he yawned, slept, chewed his bone and caught the ball, and I believe he knew how much I needed to explore his way of being.

## CHAPTER SEVEN

# AT HOME

This was where I found myself, with my family and my Four-Legs in the first few years of my new life in Sydney. I'd had no clue before we moved here that I would be rethinking, redefining and reinterpreting my whole world, and all because of a dog whose own world consisted of our home, the nearby streets, the parks and the veterinary hospital.

In his reborn life, Max found out that home was where he could have comfort and security. He would not have to fend for himself, and never have to worry about hunger or thirst or finding a comfortable place to sleep at night, even when the thunder was roaring outside. All good things in life would be provided. However, he still had decisions to make, for his choices were plenty, ranging from resting on the cool floor of the bathroom to tucking himself into a human bed among the plump cushions in the guest room in the middle of the night. Max knew instinctively what was best for him, and we often pretended not to notice his rule-breaking behaviour.

When Max first arrived there was a period of boundaries: he was clearly shown where they were and he tried his best not to cross them. I well remember his frantic face on hearing our laughter from the other side of the house while he stood there with his four paws firmly planted just at the entrance to the forbidden area, not daring to move an inch further. How much I admired his self-restraint at that young age. This was in our first house: with its clear corridor leading to the bedrooms, it was easy to clearly specify the 'human only' rooms.

Eighteen months later we moved to our present house, in which the rooms are not clearly separated by hallways or corridors. Before we found the energy to think about setting up any 'no-go' areas, Max simply took for granted that he had been advanced in his rights as a valuable family member, with the result that he immediately did away with all physical boundaries. During all these boundary-free years in this house, no one has ever protested. The fact was that we never really tried to set up new restrictions, either because we felt obliged to reward him for his previous good behaviour or because our love for him had increased enormously and therefore we granted him this extra allowance. As it turned out, he often made use of his freedom to sit in our bathrooms, watching us perform our ablutions, curious about what makes us different. I've always suspected that this must have greatly satisfied his instinct to 'spy and detect'.

Max also soon realised that home was the centre of relationships, both between our human family and, more intriguingly, between the two-legs and the four-legs. After having observed both our communication and our physical movements, he quickly understood how we related to one another, how our daughter belonged to us and needed to be protected. He could clearly sense the intimate connection, and feel the strong love of our family. As for him, our relationship clearly started out as owner and owned, but this soon turned into parents and adoptive child, quickly followed by the more elevated position of dear friend and, finally, inseparable companion, being so much loved that he became the very centre of the family within the first few years of our life together.

For my daughter, Max became her big brother, creative playmate and best friend, while my husband, being the largest person and male, was instantly recognised as the real boss in the family. He never had to talk much to communicate with Max. He only ever needed to move his eyes and give a slight whistle— an almost silent command—to receive instant obedience. This perfect understanding was reached without spoken language, and probably through body language alone. Max would watch his big boss all the time, and before he became very old he was always ready to perform whatever duties were required, be it chasing away the ducks from the swimming pool, fetching a newspaper or—and this may be difficult to believe—drinking water on command. His eagerness to obey was incredible.

During the long periods of my husband's absence from home I became the person in charge. Max understood the change of role and acted accordingly, although he was smart enough to see the difference. In order to gain his cooperation, I found myself trying hard to please him, acting more as his playmate and companion than his mistress. My overwhelming motherly love must have annoyed him at times, especially when he was having a quiet time, but these minor conflicts were soon resolved by our mutual acceptance of and concern for each other. During this time of mostly one-to-one companionship, Max and I both learned to adjust to living together. We were quick to reward each other for the good deeds and slow to show dislikes or annoyance. We shared our passion for anything playful and amusing, and we often prepared our delighted hearts together to pick up my daughter from school, welcome my husband back home, or entertain guests. We kept learning from one another, enjoying all the good things together in life. I have been amazed how a simple relationship could have developed so quickly into something so intricate and deep.

From the beginning we knew that good training would be essential for harmony at home, and in the first two years we accomplished all the basic training necessary for a well-behaved dog. Max quickly grasped such basic routines as sit and stay, fetch and drop, go and catch, wait and see. He was taught to obey orders, to the extent that, having now learned self-discipline, he would pee and poo on command with a fair degree of success. He also learned to refuse temptations outside the home, restraining himself from crossing a road to greet an old friend or picking up an inviting piece of sausage in the park. Indeed, during those formative years, he always tried his best to follow orders and achieve what was asked of him. He liked to be trained, loved to be challenged, enjoyed adventures and longed for excitement, and we, being very loving parents, created many games to satisfy his desires.

With a young and energetic dog, there were many opportunities for training that we tried to incorporate with play. One of Max's favourite games was hide and seek, and he soon learned that he had to sit and wait until we'd hidden ourselves before coming to find us. We often set up a game to be played whenever Max was left at home on his own. To keep him active, we would hide treats for him to find later, and were always amazed to see him sitting patiently and calmly watching us hide them. We knew he understood that this was a game to be played later by himself. Max's intelligence was clearly there to be seen.

Being quick-minded and innovative, Max considered home a never-ending resource for fun, and before he suffered his first stroke, he had his own ideas for play. When we put away his ball, he would bring us a piece of fruit, a leaf or a small twig that had fallen from a tree in the hope that we'd throw it for him to catch. And in the evening, as I was brushing my teeth, he would come into the bathroom and wait for his duckie, a yellow rubber duckie that accompanied my daughter in her bath when she was small. When squeezed, the duckie made a little quacking sound which fascinated Max. And even when

I had no mood to play, I still had to show him his much-loved toy. When I told him, 'Duckie is already sleeping, you also go to sleep now,' he would knowingly leave the bathroom and climb into his bed. To him, everything was interesting and had the potential to be turned into a game. His home was never boring, and we were not to feel bored either, or so he thought. It was his job to bring happiness, and often, in the process of entertaining him, we would find ourselves laughing loudly, not quite sure who was actually amusing whom.

Max also regarded himself as our security guard, and aside from the daily routines of walking and playing, he was constantly conscious of his important job to keep the house safe from intruders of any kind. Even in his deepest sleep his ears were pricked to catch the slightest sound, although it might just be a neighbour passing by in the street. He checked all tradesmen and deliverymen, sniffed visitors familiar and strange, and was especially intrigued by anyone carrying another creature's scent. He scrutinised our faces, and our slightest concern would be a signal for him to bark, or maybe even to attack, although this never happened.

Max's detective duties extended to even the smallest things in his path. He had excellent eyesight and he could see the tiniest black dot on a ceiling or wall. When he had nothing more exciting to do he would search the house for small nuisances like flies and moths or check out the garden for geckos and snails. He would watch them, but not with an appetite; then he would alert us, barking and yelping to show us that he was faithful to his duty, and it wouldn't end until we got rid of the intruders. This was usually the highlight of his day, instructing us to fulfil our duty while he stood by, excited, ready and eager to give us a helping hand. I often puzzled about this obsession with the small creatures, and observing his frenzy, wondered what might have been going on in his head, if there was more than his instincts at work. At first I thought all dogs behaved like this until other dog owners told me that they had never seen this trait. Perhaps this was Max's way of engaging with us, that by our joint efforts in dealing with these undesirables, he would be truly a part of us.

Yet he also knew how to welcome guests. He would bring out his stuffed toys for children, and for adults he would show off his other treasures, never forgetting his dirty, worn-out, plastic bone. This he would fetch from nowhere and then position himself with it, right in the middle of the party, chewing on it fervently to show us what a serious hobby he occupied himself with. Was this simply attention seeking or was he really bringing out his best to entertain our guests? But why was it always his smelly old bone? And how did he understand that the children would like the toys and not his bone, and then proceed to sometimes steal my daughter's old teddy to offer them as a gift? My psychologist friend could see right away that Max had a complex personality, and I rather think that his passion for life made him a little weird.

What really annoyed Max most were the stray cats that came creeping into our garden at night. This direct attack on his territory really drove our good-natured Four-Legs crazy, and every now and then he would stage a 'chase and catch'.

On those full-mooned, starry nights, I would see our well-tamed pet dashing towards the intruders like a gust of wind stirring up the quiet air. The near darkness blurred his features but his sharp white teeth showed his determination. Putting aside his good manners, he would charge towards his target with deadly anger, and in that I could see in him a fierce beast following his instinct to fight and kill. It must be hard for domesticated animals to suppress their innate nature, but every now and then we would have a glimpse of what was perhaps Max's original character. Why those cats were not scared and kept coming back, I do not quite understand. Maybe the same fighting spirit was in them, too. Our enthusiastic fighter, however, had to learn that size was not always an advantage. He was not always fast enough for these streetwise interlopers, but until he became very old he never neglected his duty or gave up trying.

Another nuisance was the possums that would also come in at night to climb around in our trees and audaciously feed on the bananas. Max's long nose could smell them even from inside, and he would sometimes sit up all night to spy on them. During the seasons when those protected animals were especially active, we would be woken up almost every night by his fierce barking. I often had to give him a lecture on our earnest desire for sleep and the consequence of noise pollution, but of course that was pushing the limits of his self-discipline to the very edge.

Max was always there. As soon as he woke he went to find us. And we in turn found his presence clear and solid, as he stretched on the floor, scratched his belly on the rug, yawned on the staircase, accompanied us as we cooked, or watched us as we bathed ourselves . . . He would appear from nowhere, moving around the house as if glued to a backdrop, clearly the signature of our home. Even when he was having a nap the sound of his breathing was in the air, and everywhere he went, the scent from his thick coat was unmistakable. I sometimes spent my day working in the study and every hour, he would come in to check on me and say hello, just to take a look to make sure I was still there and in good shape, then quietly go away so that I would not be distracted.

Whenever Max had to stay overnight in the veterinary hospital for a procedure, we immediately felt that something was missing: the empty garden, the rumpled dog bed, the untouched toys and the stillness in the air, all reminded us that he was not home. It seemed if he was absent, home was not complete. But he was very much more than just a physical presence in our home, he was part of its emotional and psychological fabric. He was there to support, to assist, or simply to witness. This acute sense of duty and instinctive need to join in and participate was truly remarkable, and yet he was never intrusive. Sometimes he would retreat into the background; at other times he would walk right into the midle of us, always discreet enough not to be in our way.

And whenever we were caught up in the madness of life's demanding situations, rushing about and raising our voices in annoyance or anger, out of the corner of my eye I would catch an image of our dog, watching, contemplating, perhaps even pondering our human foibles. In times of upset and distress, he soothed and calmed us in his own way, since, for him, restoring peace to our home was of the utmost importance. It was incredible how he understood his role of mediator: by standing between the conflicting parties and pacing left and right, he tried his best to bring them together. He had a sensitive heart for the weak and showed his sympathy by stretching out his big tongue and showering them with kisses. Our arguments were often halted by this silly behaviour, and we ended up laughing at him. He would just give a shrug—he didn't mind that one bit.

What Max did mind was being left alone in the house. I explained to him many times what shopping meant, and indeed he understood this, especially when I came back with his beef and chicken, but he was still always sad when we left the house. So heartbroken was he that he would climb into his bed and not watch us leave. In the first year, we simply thought the best solution was to leave him in the garden so he could find enough things there to amuse himself. We believed that it was normal for dogs to be left outside whenever their owners were out, but Max found all sorts of ways to get out of the garden and escape to the street—he simply refused to consider 'alone in the garden' as being at home. One afternoon we came back and found him sitting near the front gate waiting for us. Another time, our neighbour rang our mobile phone to tell us they had spotted an anxious Max walking in our street. We discovered a big hole dug in the garden that had led him to the front yard of the neighbouring house and from there he had made it to the street—trying to find us. After a few escapes, we understood that it was enormously important for him not to feel abandoned, so we just let him stay indoors whenever we went out. This way he still felt *at home*.

I often asked myself why he hadn't learned that there was nothing to worry about for we always returned. Was it just because he would be by himself? But then, when I thought deeper, I realised his tortured heart could never allow him to be sure we would definitely be back. It was his total devotion to us that made him so fragile. Besides, he had been betrayed before when he was sent to the RSPCA. That experience seemed to have confirmed to him that there was no certainty in life. But whenever we came back home he was there to excitedly greet us at the door, holding no grudge; and as we sometimes returned frustrated and exhausted by the outside world, he brought comfort and delight simply by being there.

When it was his turn to go out with us on his twice daily walks, he moved with exhilaration as though he was about to go to the biggest event on earth. Whereas we humans constantly demand more of the new and tend to feel bored by repetition, dogs are content with just the routine and the minimum. Max demonstrated to me how easily a pure soul can find happiness.

We have all learned there is nothing like home. For Max, enclosed by four walls and with a solid roof above to shelter from storms and enemies, with a garden outside to lie in, a cabinet full of tasty edibles, several cushions and a blanket to make a comfortable bed, enough toys around to satisfy his need for play, and, of course, the three loving members of his family to readily see to his needs, home was paradise. No matter how absorbed he was in the park, whenever we said 'Go home, Max,' he instantly left whatever he was involved in and turned to the car. He surely knew what was most important, as did we. It was where simple joy was found, with that honest heart diffusing contentment upon us. For us, Max was *home*.

CHAPTER EIGHT

# AT THE
# PARK

It wasn't long after we started our life together that we knew our pet was a real adventurer. While home was a comfortable and peaceful haven, the outside world was a constant thrill, so full of activities, adventures, risks and even danger. Max was an explorer, and his daily outings were opportunities to feel and enjoy life to the full. He welcomed challenges, longed for new tasks, was always on the lookout for surprises and never shied away from obstacles. Whether it was taking a walk in the street or playing ball in the park, Max was absolutely serious about his outings. And so were we.

To Max the park was a magical place, and as soon as we were in sight of its vast green sward his eyes would shine and his legs would take off. While I stood and watched, he would run around, roll on the wonderful scents he found and leave his own here and there, participate in the beauty of nature and revel in the sheer joy of being alive and healthy. This was a place for exercise, for training and most of all, for playing ball. He adored his small green tennis ball; it was his greatest passion. Every time we went to the park we would play his simple tennis game, where one of us would hit the ball with a tennis racquet as far as we could and he would run to catch it and bring it back.

In the beginning we'd known nothing about playing ball with dogs, for we'd never seen people doing this in Hong Kong. It was only when we noticed Max watching another dog chasing a ball and trying to join in that we found out this was how devoted parents here entertained their beloved four-legged children. From that day on, we took a tennis racquet and a ball with us to the park, and that round, green, bouncy object never failed to cast its spell on us all. Over those years I have marvelled at how much Max saw in his dirty little green ball: how he could sit and look at it for hours, intoxicated.

It might have been the speed at which the ball moved from place to place, requiring immediate action from the canine player, or simply because it bounced so well that its unpredictability could cause surprise; whatever the reason, what captivated Max was the challenge, one that he was only too ready to accept. The ball represented a powerful unknown force, even a potential danger, and he was fully satisfied in catching, containing and controlling it. And it was fun. Other dogs were most unwelcome to join in this activity, and those who tried risked a quick bite.

Cry 'Catch it,' and see Max dashing out as the ball soared into the air, coming down to land this way or that. Before the strike he would have positioned himself to judge exactly in which direction the racquet was pointing. Having ascertained this he would move towards the ball, his intense eyes fixed on it, one paw raised to be ready to go, ears upright and mouth tightly closed; he had only one target. His mind was set on this task: for him, this was a serious business, far more than just a game. Indeed, he once risked drowning himself because of his obsession with the ball. During one of our early games of catch in a small nearby park, the ball hit a tree and bounced over a low wall into Sydney Harbour. Max, then just a teenager full of energy and ready for anything regardless of the risk, saw the ball go over the wall and jumped straight after it. It was a big shock, for he hadn't expected to end up in the harbour: unlike other dogs, he didn't like water at all and had never swum before.

In this game of the tennis ball, the relationship between owner and dog is clearly established: one serves and the other retrieves; one acts and the other reacts. This requires a high level of cooperation, an absolute willingness to give and to take. In the process of learning how to adjust and adapt to their separate roles, their sensitivity towards each other's movements, inclinations, likes and dislikes is heightened, and as a consequence they come to know each other better. Despite all the drama of this high-level activity and his focus on the ball, Max never failed to follow orders or allowed his devotion to the game to carry him away. Even at his very young age, we had only to say: 'This is the last one,' for him to understand and accept that his mission for that day was over.

I have always been intrigued by how easily dogs in a park can identify one another by just a look or a smell. As soon as we stopped playing catch, Max would go straight off to spend some time with the other paws who shared the playground with him. Carefully avoiding any enemies in his path, he would first run to greet his friends before joining in more intimate greetings. He would teach a quick lesson to a dog with an odd smell, or who was perhaps misbehaving, by pinning it down to show it what strength meant. Although I don't believe he ever meant to hurt, he could make his dog companions yelp. Sometimes he would give the little terriers with hair covering their eyes quite a scare—they would curl down on the ground as if asking for mercy when they spotted him marching into the park.

Like humans, Max instantly showed his preferences with his kind. He would never try any tricks on poodles, as if he knew how easily he could be outsmarted, while greyhounds seemed too restless for him to take much pleasure in their company. As for bulldogs, he very soon learned about their dislike of other four-legged animals after an unexpected fight with one of the more aggressive of the breed. This had taught him that the best way to protect himself from these bullies was to avoid all close encounters with them. The full-breed German shepherd had to be handled with respect. Max knew very well why they were chosen for police work (he'd perhaps heard of that clever German television detective Inspector Rex), which would explain why, whenever he saw one of those really big and brawny creatures, he would simply turn around and move off in another direction. Why risk a fight when you are likely to be the loser? Boxers and chow-chows were also to be greeted from a distance, as if closer contact might bring bad luck. This sudden caution always amused me after all that intimate body touching with his favourite companions.

With the loyal labradors and golden retrievers, he would usually go up to them and just say hello, enthusiastically but discreetly so as not to distract them from their owners. He was especially interested in cattle dogs, kelpies and border collies, probably because they belonged to the same rural group, all of them either sheep or cattle herders. They seemed very fond of him and tried hard to stir him up to play. But Max was often hesitant to join in their game for he rather liked to walk or jog with me.

The dogs moved so fast, running around chasing each other or catching and fetching, that I was worried they might knock me over, but they never did. They would miss me, sometimes by a mere whisker, and as I watched I would laugh at what a scene it was—crazy dogs, playing hard, checking out other dogs, living life to the full and just enjoying the moment; dogs in all shapes, colours and sizes, from huge to miniature, from smart and alluring and to odd-looking with funny, squashed-in faces. I loved seeing how they all socialised, acted and reacted, putting so much life on display.

As a new arrival from the concrete jungle of Hong Kong, all this was totally new. It was hard to remember that until I met Max, I'd been afraid of dogs.

We dog lovers are a special kind, our lives either partly or largely determined by our dogs. Year after year we would meet in the park: dog parents and their four-legged children. We would stop to say hello, exchange a few dog stories (inevitably praising our own yet remaining ever mindful of showing proper appreciation of the other dogs) and then we would walk on our way. Rain or sunshine, we would find ourselves dedicated to our duty. Somehow, the very presence of so many other dog lovers was an encouragement, a reminder that we were not alone, that our personal commitment to our four-legged friends was witnessed by and shared with many others. From the moment we stepped into the park and caught sight of one another we would feel strengthened by some unspoken support. We'd be reassured that it was not a strange fancy to be so faithful to our dogs and that we were all just normal people with hearts big enough for creatures other than humans.

Yet even though we were connected we were still apart, for we were not there for ourselves, but for our dogs. Rarely did we talk about other aspects of our lives: if one of us was absent we would wonder what had happened to their dog. One day I met again the elderly owner of a good-natured bull-terrier who used to be Max's friend. She told me that her family had moved and that she had come back for a visit. Her first response to my greeting was to reassure me that her beloved pet was still alive, although now much too frail for the long journey to Sydney. As we said goodbye I realised that I knew a lot about her dog but very little about her, and that we were linked only by our inter-species relationships. I wondered: were we perhaps too single-minded in our focus on our four-legged friends?

The park was a major part of Max's life, where he could show what it meant to be a free spirit, running, chasing, jumping, catching, fighting: he was action on display, the very expression of vitality and life itself. We went to the park to enjoy an experience we could not find elsewhere, a period of play and fun that showed us the lighter, softer side of living in a big city. In summer, we risked being burnt by the blazing sun and, even with a breeze to soothe our bodies and souls, we walked with sweat crawling down our foreheads. Winter was entirely different. In the early mornings, and wrapped in our heavy jackets, we gulped down the icy air, grateful we were alive and well. Stepping on the crisp yellow leaves, we thought about the passage of seasons and the transience of everything. Rainy days were not pleasant for walking, but made us all sentimental. And the stormy days of dark skies and thunder, though scary for our pets, touched us in their own way.

Every day was its own. We noticed the change of the wind, the smell in the air, trees growing taller, flowers blooming and then dying, fledgling birds learning to fly, thousands of beetles, millions of ants, and our fellow humans and their dogs growing up and becoming old. To us, such a world with our dogs was more open, more interesting but it was also more intricate, too. There were differences and distinctions as well as untold similarities. We embraced life, and shared with one another the beauty of all things and the meaning of relationships between humans and animals.

Together with the fitness trainers, lone joggers, loving couples, elderly men and women, small children and babies in their prams, we were part and parcel of the life of the park. Simply being there made the beginning of our days lively and cheerful, and their ending peaceful and tender.

This is what I could never have envisaged while I was living in Hong Kong, any more than my relatives and friends there can now. There are few real parks in Hong Kong and people don't normally walk in them, so they cannot imagine what it is like to play outdoors with a dog. Expecting them to understand what my life in the park has given me is simply asking too much.

When I see those poor dogs in Hong Kong walking on hard pavements, surrounded by impatient pedestrians and breathing in polluted air from the congested traffic, I do so pity them. How they must have to endure discomfort to obey their human masters. How truly self-sacrificing but sadly helpless they are.

## CHAPTER NINE

# A SPECIAL
# DOG

Even though he sniffed and played ball like the other dogs, somehow my Four-Legs always stood out from the crowd. I used to think he was special in my eyes only, until other dog owners told me that he was unique. People in the park and along the local streets would follow us or stop walking or playing to inspect him. Even the customers at pavement cafés would turn their heads to look at him as we went by. Some even hurried across busy roads to ask about him, wanting a closer look at this 'magnificent creature'. Everywhere we went people were so attracted by his charm they just couldn't help staring at him—and how they loved to stroke him. Enticed by his smart looks, even the mean-spirited would squeeze out a smile for him, and over the years I have seen many a gloomy face brightened when Max naively offered his ball, asking for a game. I, too, regularly paused to look at him during our walks. More and more I found myself entranced in my admiration of his beauty and liveliness.

For Max the outside world was always a place of goodwill, of kind and friendly gestures. He would proudly present his beautiful smile, leaving no doubt that he believed it was wonderful to have four legs, to attract so much attention and to bring delight to so many. He kept particular watch over the children in the park, offering his ball even to the littlest ones sitting in their prams, and their parents understood and appreciated his good intentions. Old people who walked with difficulty would give the ball a kick to please him, and it always made me laugh when athletic types working hard at their training would stop in the middle of their routines to throw it for him. When he was in an especially good mood he could be very generous with his kisses, so that sunbathing or napping strangers were at risk of being given a quick one. I wondered why they weren't ever angry about being disturbed in this manner, for Max never gave up easily. I never saw anyone look annoyed nor heard them complain about my dog's intrusive behaviour.

Max seemed to think that everyone should be playing and having fun, and his persistence to share the good things in life was indeed impressive. There were so many people ready to join him, and they never minded being called to attention by his charming innocence. He seemed instinctively aware of how far he could go. It was incredible how seldom he got this wrong, how his assumptions about people so rarely let him down. I regularly told myself he had found the wrong guy, but to my surprise, the object of Max's attention would pick up that dirty, smelly ball to play with a totally determined dog. His naive persistence would bring out the best in even the most unapproachable person. Until he showed me otherwise, I'd had no idea that this was possible.

It was as though Max had been born with a talent to connect with humans, and there were times when it felt as though he believed he was one of us. As he matured in years and understanding, he often preferred to be an observer of the canine activities at the park, happy just to stand and watch over the other dogs as they played, chased and fought. He was delighted to be around them, overseeing and perhaps cheering them on, interested but participating in spirit only. I long suspected that the reason he stopped playing with other dogs was that he had come to feel he was not one of them. I was convinced from the way he moved around them and the way he looked at us, that he considered himself to belong to the human race.

There have always been a few views about Max's origins. To the RSPCA he was a German shepherd–border collie cross, but I suppose this was only a guess, for the staff we spoke to didn't think this was the case. While the German shepherd side was obvious from the bushy tail and Max's telltale black patch, it was his almost orange coat that marked him out as a dingo. In Hong Kong we'd never heard of these native Australian wild dogs, so from the moment we brought Max home I was surprised by the interest shown in the dingo connection.

We noticed how people looked at him and we heard them refer to him as a dingo, even by young children who would call out excitedly, 'Look, there's a dingo!' A number of dingo owners assured me that our handsome boy was at least half dingo, while other equally expert dog owners have asserted with the same certainty that he possessed traits of kelpie and cattle dog. Some have even said his ancestry was Finnish spitz or half husky. He's been called 'Wolfy' and 'Foxy', but to the people in the park he was always 'Gorgeous'.

Hardly a day has gone by without my being reminded of what a remarkable dog I possess. Even at his old age now, he continues to give pleasure and make heads turn. It is not uncommon for me to be greeted by strangers in the street or at the supermarket. They all remember me only because of my special dog.

We have become famous, my Four-Legs and me, and I cannot hide my pride.

## CHAPTER TEN

# AT THE VET HOSPITAL

For Max and me, not all of our outings have been entirely pleasant. Full of surprises and requiring a lot of endurance, visits to the vet hospital were unavoidable, but they have provided an opportunity to observe how the interaction between animal children and their human parents is managed through body language, signs and sounds.

Max was born with a few congenital problems: skin rashes, tummy upsets, cysts, lumps and even cancer, so visits to the vet became a regular business. And as he has aged, arthritis has also become a major concern. Although he has never refused to walk inside the vet hospital, he is not good at hiding his apprehension. With a serious face, bushy tail erect, eyes alert and sharp, he knows to prepare himself for the unexpected. While never exactly worried, for he trusts whatever we do for him, he constantly checks my face and listens attentively, trying to catch any familiar sounds. I watch him, too, trying to comprehend what it must be like to surrender oneself completely to another being.

While we sit and wait our turn, other animals come and go, each as uptight as Max, and I think it must be like gambling with one's destiny. These poor souls don't know how they are going to be treated. Dogs in vet hospitals all behave differently and unlike their park manner, none of them dares initiate a fight or a confrontation—it's as though they know that significant events are taking place in their lives. They seem to understand the purpose of visiting this place. Max is always quick to show interest in the other dogs, but more as if wanting to find out what's wrong with them.

The nurse's cat sometimes roams freely in the reception area. She is cheeky and smart with an arrogant flair, and shows no sign of fear as she watches the animals come and go. Max has a grudge against cats and one of his most basic instincts is to threaten them, but he walks in and out of the hospital with his eyes straight ahead, although his nose and ears are always fully alert for any sign of feline misbehaviour. Even when the cat walks past, he holds himself back, behaving as if it were just another dog: no stirring, no agitation. Once, he and the cat sat facing each other for almost fifteen minutes without the slightest sign of annoyance. Max was determined to outsmart the cat by simply ignoring her. I was surprised by this self-control. It required at least an understanding and calculation of the consequences of bad behaviour on his part.

Often from behind a closed door we can hear the sound of whimpering or a few hollow woofs of complaint. Max frowns: he understands. Misfortune does happen in this place, and sometimes truly sad suffering. One time, a yelping, fluffy snow white dog was led by the staff into the operating room. Max spotted the owner's red eyes and heard her repeated words, 'My good girl, be brave, it will soon be over.' My kind-hearted boy was so touched he almost tried to offer a kiss of comfort. Once we've stepped inside he knows he is earmarked mostly for an unpleasant experience.

Sometimes Max gets nervous. He shows this by turning around and trying to find a place to settle, putting his head between my legs or even trying to climb onto my lap. After a while he will quietly sit down, although his head keeps turning left and right, watching, and his ears are perked up, listening. He waits patiently for his bad luck. To me, this is true courage, to be ready for and receptive to the unknown.

Max knows this is the place to go in order to get well. He never puts up a fight, although it means discomfort and endurance, sometimes even having to stay away from home for a few hours or even overnight.

I can tell that Max recognises the professionals here. He exhibits a certain heightened respect, and puts on his best behaviour. And he never forgets to give his big generous smile. 'He's the happiest dog I've ever seen,' a vet once said, and

I believed she wasn't just trying to please me. Her own smile showed me this. 'How wonderful Max is,' I told myself. He knows the vet is trying to help, whether it's by inserting the needle, checking his teeth or examining a wound, there is a purpose and therefore trust.

If he has to stay for a procedure, I assure him I will be back. He stares deeply into my eyes and he knows I will return to take him home. And when I do reappear he lights up, and pulls his body together and takes big steps towards me to show his gratitude for not being abandoned again. Bliss, a sudden surging bliss. I can tell he has only one thing on his mind: going home.

I too dread going to the vet hospital. When Max was diagnosed with a cancerous paw, the word 'cancer' struck me so hard that I couldn't follow what the vet was saying. I was so worried I wanted to ask Max what we should do, but his wide eyes looked back at me, as if to say: 'Whatever you decide, I trust you.' Yes, he trusts me. But it is this very trusting that bothers me.

The vet asked me: 'Do you know how to inject the liquid into his mouth?' I knew for sure that, unless my boy was super-cooperative, I was not going to do it well. I did try my best, but Max kept his mouth tightly shut. We sat down quietly facing each other, and he eyed me, saying: 'No, don't try anymore, you're not going to succeed. I hate that stuff.' Just as he hated swallowing his medication, Max refused to stop pulling out the stitches of his surgery wound. I had been warned, but Max's bleeding open wound told the vet all he needed to know: the

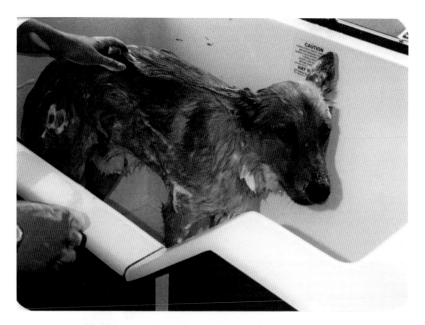

more I ordered Max to stop pulling at the stitches, the more he ignored me.

Sometimes we assume too readily as pet owners that we can handle animals. I am not pretending ignorance when the vet confronts me with explanations of causes and outcomes I do not understand. In moments of doubt I seek assurance from Max in the hope that he has listened carefully to the vet's instructions. There have also been times when I've not been clear enough in my explanations of Max's sickness, so the vet has turned to him directly to find out the problem. Max can only follow me and trust in my good intentions, but I know he doesn't believe all that I say.

Every visit to the vet hospital is an opportunity for me to form a clearer picture of Max's state of health and well-being: what is at risk, whether there is a need for preventive measures or how to prepare for some time bomb that may be about to explode. Age is generally the decisive factor. With every consultation I learn a bit more about the health issues that affect dogs: their illnesses, diseases and allergies and the complications of treatment. I am reminded again how precious the lives of these animal children are.

I have so often stepped into the vet's surgery ready to be told the worst, only to step out again with the affirmation of life together. Max and I then walk away with lively strides, even more conscious of what it means to share our life together, of the shortness and fragility of life and the brevity of most animal–human relationships.

When I see those frail, old animals dragging their aging bodies towards the vet and the tears running down their owners' faces, I know this is a place where hearts are either burdened and wounded from seeing the failing side of life or are full of gratitude for the gift of life. The veterinary hospital is not a place for the faint-hearted; it is a place where every decision matters for the keeping or ending of a life. Here you come close to understanding what it means to hold life in your hands. You also know that one day you are going to have to face the same dreadful decision yourself, the choice between life and death. It is the ultimate power, yet at the same time you realise how powerless, in fact, we all are.

The agonising question that so often faces loving pet parents is: when is the right time to stop the suffering of an animal who is also your best friend? Which is harder: to stop their suffering by quickly ending their lives with just one needle, or to retaining and cherishing every available moment together but with the anguish of your best friend's ever-increasing pain? I believe that most animals do want to go on—after all, survival is their most basic instinct, and they have the most exceptional ability to endure pain, usually suffering in silence. Whatever the decision, the torment in the heart is real.

Max and I do not take these trips to the vet easily, even though we are usually prepared for what is to come. He understands that this may be an ordeal, but it is all part of the game of staying alive. But as soon as we arrive back home he collapses into his basket, buries his ears among the pillows and always lets out a heavy sigh. That big job of self-discipline, obedience, courage and trust is now over. It takes a lot of energy, this cooperation with uncertainty.

Taking a human child to the doctor is not quite the same. Children soon let you know where the pain is and what they need, and after a certain age the doctor can communicate directly with the child. Even though you may not totally understand your child's complaint, you do know what it means to have a tummy ache or a sprained ankle. And most important of all, you can usually talk your child into accepting medication or other treatments at home. The doctor trusts you as a parent and you readily give assurance of your parental capability.

Why is it that a normally confident person is nervous about handling a sick dog? Is it because Max depends on me totally or is it because I am only human and only know about human things? Often Max and I would come home from the vet exchanging stressed looks. I knew how he dreaded the tedious procedures and he knew how I dreaded them too. I can only rely on my own common sense to decide what's best for my four-legged friend. It's because I care so much about him and am so worried and troubled that I become so unsure and hesitant. The love Max and I have is so great that I become fragile and weak when he is unwell. The simple fact is that we are so different, but I am determined to look after him as best as I can. Surely Four-Legs knows it, too.

It is with mixed feelings, wholehearted dedication but lacking self-confidence, that I have found myself so often at the vet hospital. I come in with a serious face, a frown between my eyes and so many prepared questions. Sometimes I lose patience and leave the hospital promising that I will try my best. From these diligent animal savers, young men and women who dare to show their love and compassion for non-humans and who are always understanding and sympathetic to the worried animal parents, I learn what kindness truly means and what a big heart is. I admire them and respect them, not just because their work is hard, but because I know it requires a lot more than a clever mind to be able to love those who are totally at our mercy. Every time I step out to the street and look up to the wide and far-away sky, I thank God that I have so much support and help in my role as a dog owner.

When I was in Hong Kong visiting my mother, Max suffered a stroke so severe that he couldn't stand. My daughter arranged for our sympathetic vet to come to our house to see Max. So concerned was he that he took Max to his home and let him sleep on the floor next to his bed. I was so terrified, but the vet assured me that Max would receive the best possible care. He said: 'I know Max is very important to you and I'll treat him like my own dear dog. Don't worry.' When I arrived home, Max was already able to greet me with a warm welcome, although he struggled to come close with his wobbly walk. How grateful I was to this kind man, and by extension all those whose love for animals takes them so far beyond the boundaries of the normal professional relationship.

A few days later, at the specialist vet hospital, I sat with Max waiting to be called. I was no longer devastated. I knew with absolute certainty that the vets and nurses here would do their best to save him, that this was a place where animals drew out the very best from their human carers. It was a wonderful thing, this near-perfect interaction between dog and human.

## CHAPTER ELEVEN

# A NEW IDENTITY

From the earliest days, both my husband and my daughter were amazed by my newfound devotion to Max and the way he had helped me to adjust to our new life in Australia. I do believe it was a relief for them to know that he would be well cared for when they weren't around. As time goes by, they have become convinced that I am the most dedicated dog mother and happy to be one. They need never be worried about the wellbeing of this fourth member of our family.

My husband has never failed to show love and care for his adopted animal son, but for much of the time only from long distance, as his life has unexpectedly turned out to be far from downsized. Although semi-retired from his garment business, he has taken on other work and activities overseas, as if life should be filled with as much as possible before it recedes and finally disappears. He also has to attend to the needs of his elderly mother in Germany, so at best he can only be a part-time father to Max, although he continues to give instructions over the phone. My daughter's busy schedules and demanding young-adult lifestyle, on the other hand, require her full concentration for most of the time, so that early promise to walk her 'big brother' has become an impossibility. I certainly hadn't foreseen this on the day I signed the adoption paper at the RSPCA. So, as I watch this young girl spread her wings and soar up into young womanhood, with her many friends and activities, I just quietly take up the leash and go out walking with my boy.

I know that both my husband and daughter love their dog and think of him a lot, and I also believe that he is still my daughter's best companion, even though she now spends so little time with him. When everyone is at home there is no doubt that Max is the focus of our family. We pay the most attention to him and enjoy being with him, playing, talking or just having fun, and he doesn't mind at all being the enter-tainer of the family. We are touched by the joy he has given us, and we all recognise him as our wonderful blessing.

But increasingly I find myself alone with Max. The world is so complex and overwhelming that it is easy to neglect those aspects of it that do not require urgent attention or give instant gratification. There are always more important matters needing to be done, including, certainly, the self to be nurtured and satisfied, so a dog at home can wait. Indeed, Max waits faithfully for the intimate contacts with his dearest human sister and for his great master to reappear. When he was younger, he would put his treasured bone on my husband's pillow from time to time, perhaps thinking that this was the least he could do to please a faraway master. When I first discovered the bone and talked to him about it, he was quite embarrassed, but still his dedication has never faltered.

Perhaps the certainty of their dogs' love and loyalty makes humans less concerted in their efforts to be with them. Is this because we generally don't love our animals enough to overlook ourselves? Do I have the right to hold these people responsible for not fulfilling their roles as animal owners or am I the abnormal one, expecting too much of others simply because I ask so much of myself? Since bringing Max home, I have carried out my vow to devote a considerable part of my life to my dog while at the same time being fully engaged as a wife, mother and housewife. Have I neglected myself while others have been busy pursuing their own interests? Have I been making a fool of myself? Perhaps it's because my family knows they can rely on me entirely that they don't feel a need to commit. Whenever these questions pop up as I stay quietly alone at home to keep Max company, his eyes always give me an assurance that is not only strengthening but heartening. I am very content to be with him, even though it means missing out on pursuing other pleasures. My dog has given me so much that I am happy to sacrifice my self-interest for time with him. I have postponed trips to those 'must visit' destinations to future years when Max will no longer be at home waiting for me. This is the least I can do, to thank him for what he has given me.

In the process of carrying out Max's daily routines, caring for his physical and emotional health and adapting to his world, I have also adjusted to my new life in Sydney, liking it so much that I have become quite forgetful of my previous life in Hong Kong. Without much fuss, it seems, I have also managed to unconsciously put aside my own ego, as I realised that my new life could not succeed without certain self-sacrifice. And just as my appetite has grown for the fresh fruits and vegetables, seafood and lamb of Australia, so my ears have become attuned to the unfamiliar Australian accent. With my Australian driver's licence, I have mastered the art of living in this new place. At certain moments I did think back to how good it was in Hong Kong when I had a chauffeur to drive me around and a live-in maid to help with shopping and cooking, but I was quick to dismiss such thoughts and didn't allow myself to indulge in any regrets. I was determined that I would not just survive, but would thrive. Not surprisingly, in the first few years I did slip and fall in my attempts to adapt, and sometimes I took a wrong turn, but before I was aware, I had already called myself an Australian.

In the beginning the frustration, doubts and dread I felt were to be expected, but my new life started like the turning of a tap and just kept on running. There was so much to learn that it wasn't possible to take a break or wait until I felt strong enough. There was no time for a dress rehearsal, I just had to jump onto the stage as the curtains opened with little to support me. I was dazzled by the lights, and heard the audience growing impatient. I knew then that the time had come for me to gather my courage and play my part, to laugh and sing and mix with others. I hadn't just taken on a role, I'd now taken on a new life and was living it. In doing so I discovered a wisdom that I had never known: that it was not only hard work that produced a good life. Something as insignificant as a single hair from a furry coat was enough to remind me of the fun and delight of life.

Together with Max, I somersaulted into this unknown world so full of surprises, and to this day I am amazed at how rapidly I came to terms with the many changes in my life. It was not just the move to Sydney, the separation from my family in Hong Kong and the end of my teaching career, there were also my daughter's growing up, my husband's frequent absences and my new role as administrator of our family home and security. And there, always in the centre of the action, sat the solid presence of my new four-legged friend. He was always there, waiting for me when I came home from shopping, meetings, attending courses or dining with friends. By design or by choice, we were connected. It was my Four-Legs who gave me the extra support I needed to succeed in my new Australian life. At the time of our first encounter at the RSPCA, I was far too proud a human to appreciate this lovely animal's potential as both companion and helpmate. I'd thought only of how much I would have to sacrifice myself for him, simply because I could not envisage how this kind of bonding might be possible. How superficial I was to so under-value the capacity of a dog.

My daily practice of walking Max has taught me to under-stand the extraordinary bond that exists between humans and their animals and I delight in discussing our beloved pets with other dog owners. No matter how engaged we are in our human activities, we always have time to talk about our dogs. Now human-ness is not my only concern; dog-ness occupies an increasingly important place in my life, and this has given me a new understanding of the words 'friendship' and 're-lationship'. It is as if the world has opened up and I can see further and deeper, not just into dogs but into humans as well, and the many things that coexist in nature and life.

I do, however, understand that many people would not care for my life with Max; in fact, they would consider it too simple and unproductive. To keep a pet is commonplace and to walk a dog is nothing special, so why talk about it? But instead of swallowing your own joy, remember the beauty and charm of a four-legged creature cannot really be appreciated by those who have never experienced the happiness of owning a dog.

I used to be one of those people, listening politely but half-heartedly to dog stories while inwardly believing that these animals' ability to understand and feel was highly exag-gerated by their owners. Like other unbelievers, I thought dog lovers were either using their dogs to compensate for what was lacking in their own lives or as comfort against the misery of the world at large.

I am ashamed that I was not more respectful, that I was so

proud and arrogant in my judgement of others that I thought I could never be one of them. I now consider it humbling to be able to befriend an animal, and wonderfully satisfying to really get to know one. In my long journey of discovery, I have learned what it means to truly share my life with another species. Max didn't just make me more physically active, he also stimulated me mentally and absorbed me emotionally. He quickly converted me from a dog owner to a dog lover.

And while I'd thought in the beginning that I would be in control, I soon found that I was the one being led: instead of being human-focused our activities were Max focused. I have finally realised that what I once thought as trivial is in fact deeply significant; that life with a dog provides so much more than mere solace for the depressed soul. In a subtle way, Max was able to bring to my life new interests that had the power to invigorate and excite me. I enjoy seeing trees, touching flowers, looking at the sky and the sea, all the things that I didn't pay attention to in the past. I now see that we are all but a tiny part of creation.

By caring for Max, I have distanced myself from many of my worries and concerns. He has opened a new chapter of life, one with very little of me and plenty of him. In it I draw with colours that are both bright and dull, and write with rapture and sorrow. And on every page there are many paws and kisses as Max steps across them, shedding his warmth over my many cares.

And so I have lived these years of my immigrant life, and wherever I am and whatever I do, Max has been by my side, as my companion and my support. Whenever I am faced with frustration, his tender gaze, the weight of his head on my lap and the dampness from the touch of his nose on my skin are the only encouragement I need. They convey to me that he understands and cares. We have walked miles and miles, making our footprints on life's path. The sun has been witness to our secret sharing and the trees have heard our testimonies. It was Max who took the lead, and I have followed as he has turned my world into his world and his into mine.

Living with a dog means not only letting him be part of your life, it also means letting go yourself. I have banished forever my obsession with cleanliness and tidiness, as what I had once considered the maid's work is now my own. By bending down to clean, brush and talk to Max, I have not only lowered myself physically, I have humbled my ego. I recognise that I didn't just adopt a dog, but I adopted a dog's approach to life as well: his carefree spirit, his forgiving nature, his playful yet cheerfully persistent personality and his energy. I abandoned my pride and learned to improve myself so that I honestly believe I am now a better person. And I like who I now am. It was through Max that I have a persistence to live a fuller and more joyous life.

I didn't plan to change, it wasn't a conscious decision. I simply had no option. Walking with Max has given me courage and patience and a clearer understanding of the profound simplicity of life.

Through my dog I have undergone an amazing transformation. I now find myself opening new windows that reveal life and all its beautiful mysteries. I know that whatever may happen in the future, I will find strength from the lessons my Four-Legs has passed on to me, and that I will be able to cope with whatever is my destiny.

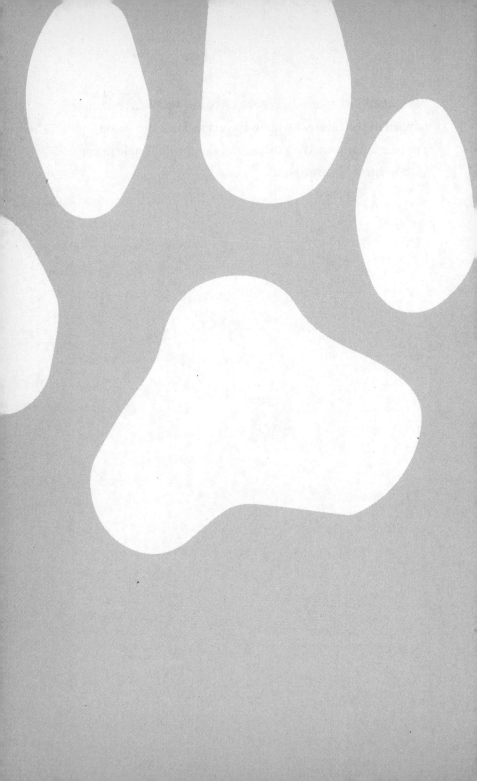

# THE
# PHILOSOPHICAL
# QUESTIONS

## CHAPTER TWELVE

# DOG CONSCIOUSNESS

I often wonder how I came to understand Max and to know his likes and dislikes so well. I talk quite comfortably about his character, his personality, his thoughts and his feelings, and I am pretty sure that most of the time he understands my commands, my words and even my feelings. But what makes me so sure? How do I know that I am not, in fact, simply deluding myself?

The philosopher, Raimond Gaita, questions dog lovers' conception of dog consciousness: what we mean when we say our dogs can understand us. In his book, *The Philosopher's Dog*, he challenges us to show him some substantial evidence justifying our claims about our dogs' consciousness, but he realises right away that there is no way we can produce that evidence, because dogs cannot tell us what they feel or whether they are thinking about something.

Even scientific knowledge of a dog's nervous system cannot give us any certainty, yet somehow we dog lovers do know, without being able to prove it, that our canine friends do not just act on instincts. We believe they are not governed merely by mechanical impulses and that there is something more, something similar to human consciousness that occurs inside them. That something is what we call 'dog consciousness'. Interestingly, Gaita's observation of his own dog has convinced him that his dog is able to feel emotional pain and joy.

With Max, I am convinced that a process resembling very simple thinking takes place in his brain for decision-making. While he is certainly led by instinct to circle around other dogs in the park, to sniff at a scent or chase after a ball, he never forgets to check on whether I am still there waiting for him or if I approve of his behaviour. I often trick him by hiding behind a tree, and as soon as I'm out of his sight he panics, stops whatever he is doing and comes to find me. To me it is obvious that he must go through some sort of thinking process in order to reach the conclusion that he has to find me, for him to understand the causal relationship between behaviour and consequence.

To take this further, I believe that it requires more than just a mechanical reaction for him to lie down in submission to allow me to dress a wound, when it obviously hurts very much and I normally don't reward him with treats afterwards. Or whenever I cough continuously and he comes to me with wide eyes to inquire about me, when there is no mistaking the worry in his face as he comes close to lick my leg, not to ask for a treat but to show his concern and love for me. It intrigues me that he seems to understand the negative connotation of coughing and, for that matter, of limping, as when I'd twisted my ankle. Dogs can observe the slightest change in our behaviour and they seem to understand the implications of something being out of the ordinary. And just as I am convinced that they are capable of making some kind of comparison between the ordinary and the unusual, I wonder if they might possibly question the what and the why.

One afternoon I was stunned by a clear demonstration of Max's 'thinking process'. His knee had been injured a month earlier, but because he'd responded so well to medication and didn't seem to still feel pain, we were back to his usual daily walk. We would jump over a narrow ditch, and it was normally my four-legged friend who led the way, leaping swiftly across and then turning his head to watch me jump. But that afternoon, as we were approaching the ditch, he slowed down and stopped. I quickly jumped over, expecting him to follow, but he turned away, looked around and walked to the road to find an alternative route. On our way back he again avoided jumping over the ditch. Some sort of calculation must have occurred in his brain at those moments: perhaps he even considered the potential damage of jumping over the ditch onto his weakened knee. I can still remember his puzzled face staring down into that ditch and then back at me, as I urged him to come over. For me, this is astonishing and not just an outcome of instinct.

So what do we mean when we claim that our dogs can think? Because we humans don't really know any cognitive functions other than our own, we can only assess our dogs by projecting human concepts on them, and thus our concepts of thoughts and feelings can complicate our understanding. Although we can never understand clearly what's going on in their brains, by close observation we know that they are much more than just a mass of physical and chemical reactions, that there is something about animals we cannot grasp.

In her popular book, *Inside of a Dog*, the cognitive scientist Alexandra Horowitz emphasises the risk of using anthropomorphism to satisfy our human desire to know our dogs. While she relates to the dog lovers' frustration at not being able to make sense of their dogs' behaviour, she also urges us to adopt the dogs', and not the human, perspective, in order to understand them better. Her assumption is that we humans are 'intrinsically prejudiced' in applying our familiar human terms and concepts such as 'loving feelings' or 'guilty consciences' to canines and other animals.

In my opinion, we shall never be able to look at things entirely from a dog's perspective, simply because we are only human and animals can't tell us how they think or why they act in certain ways. As Wittgenstein once said, 'If a lion could speak, we wouldn't understand him.' Indeed, human knowledge stalls in the face of the inner life of animals.

Even in our human world there are still many puzzles about ourselves that require further studies and a different approach from the conventional wisdom. Cognitive science about animal behaviour can only cover half of the picture: the other half is found in the understanding of those who are closely connected to the animals. Even if we have a lot of evidence to prove how dogs perceive the world by their incredibly acute senses, which are without doubt very different from our own, it still says little about how they actually feel about us, about our two worlds and about how we relate to each other.

Recent research in the United States has revealed dogs' incredible learning ability, citing the case of an especially smart border collie who has learned to recognise the names of over a thousand objects. Scientists are overwhelmed, and are now curious about the upper limits of dogs' potential to retain information.

Jeffrey Masson, the author of *Dogs Never Lie About Love*, is emphatic that we must remain humble about the inner capabilities of our canine companions, as there are many things about them we actually don't know and it is quite probable that dogs possess senses and qualities beyond human expectation and comprehension, including feeling sorrow and joy.

On the other hand, Dr David McFarland, an expert in the study of animal behaviour, points out that, as we have no access to the phenomenon of being an animal, it is thus rather more a question of philosophy than of science. He believes there is little hope that science will solve the problem of 'animal philosophy'.

This shows how much there is still to find out about our pets. As much as we want to reach into their minds to fathom the meaning of their behaviour, because we are so restricted by human concepts and perspectives, at best we can only rely on our imagination. It seems that the debate about animal consciousness may never reach a convincing conclusion.

Besides, what truly matters is the relationship: what our animals give us and how we as their masters, owners, leaders or friends perceive them, how we feel about their living with us and how we believe they think and feel about us. The concept of 'truth' is therefore not a question of science but more a matter of endless philosophical calculation. For only in a very close relationship are we able to understand, assess and judge one another—and who knows my beloved four-legged companion better than I do?

While writing this book I have been reading Elizabeth M. Thomas's *The Hidden Life of Dogs*. Thomas is more than a dog lover, she is an anthropologist who has lived with and studied a self-connected family of dogs, wolves and even a dingo for more than 30 years. Her book is a detailed account of the different characters and behaviour patterns of her animals, and she never questions whether they can think or feel, as she is absolutely convinced that her canine companions have a consciousness that can understand many things. Her close observation and immense concern for them reveals to us what conscious thinking and deep feeling these animals are capable of—in fact, she boldly calls her book 'a book about dog consciousness'.

I am encouraged to think that it is probably true that dogs do possess an individual character of their own, with particular desires and fears and a certain ability to reason, especially when given options; that they do feel about people and things in a manner similar to our human way of becoming happy or sad due to changes in circumstances. Naturally these thoughts and feelings are generated by experience: the more dogs are stimulated, the more they use their brains, and possibly the more they are able to think and feel as a result. Perhaps I can dare to believe that I have not drawn these conclusions from my own imagination.

There is no denying that dogs are not all born the same. Some are cleverer than others, and a few can learn to be thoughtful. Max is one of those who is particularly sensitive to human talk and movements and can easily understand more than basic commands. Over time he has come to know the relationship between behaviour and consequence, that if he sits still and waits long enough in front of me while I am eating, eight times out of ten I will drop something yummy on the floor for him, and all he needs to do is show me his big smile. He also knows what he is not allowed to do, things that he will only do when he's out of our sight. Many times I have watched him from around a bend in the staircase and found him doing things that he clearly knows are forbidden, like scratching the bandage on his wound or rubbing his bottom on the carpet, and when he looks up to meet my eyes he becomes embarrassed and stops right away. There is a subtlety in all these observations, and I'm quite sure that he is conscious of many other things that please or bother us.

Thomas claims that, if dogs were not able to think and feel, 'there wouldn't be any dogs'. That is to say, dogs, being such loved companions of humans, must possess extraordinary dispositions which are not often found in other animals. Otherwise, why would we give so much to them in return?

## Chapter Thirteen

# INTER-SPECIES COMMUNICATION

It is intriguing how we can communicate with dogs without speaking, by relying mainly on body language to convey our intentions. In training our dogs we make sounds with specific meanings, and it is the reiteration of these sounds, often accompanied by movements, that registers in their brains to make sense of what we want them to do. Soon the sound or the movement alone is enough. This is not to say that spoken language is not an important part of our communication, but it does show how we constantly use many other ways to relate to each other.

Max and I have excellent non-verbal communication. I know what 'tail language' means: by checking to see if his tail is low or high I can tell whether he is being submissive or aggressive. The position of his ears tells me about his alertness, and also shows his conscience, especially when he has committed an offence. Our understanding of each other is greatly facilitated by his amazing power of observation: in order to know what I want he watches me all the time, especially how my hands move and what I am holding. When I show him my forefinger he knows he has to sit, whereas my whole hand indicates wait and be still. Even what I am wearing is of interest to him, and he knows for sure that putting on my jogging shoes means we're going out for a walk. He is very good at relating my body posture to my intentions and feelings.

But it is our eyes that speak most. If we want to find out how we both are feeling, we just stare straight into each other's eyes to see whether they are widened, half-shut, bulging or filled with emotion. The eyes—the so-called 'windows to the soul'—do not need spoken language: just by gazing and staring, my dog and I seem to be able to connect at the level of our souls. But if he feels embarrassed or he has done something I disapprove of, he will avoid eye contact with me, in the same way people do.

Incredibly, silence is a wonderful way of communicating with Max. There is in life something beyond speech, an area that talking cannot unlock, a space that can only be accessed by a higher form of communication, through close contact of the eyes and the body. We reprove with a stare and wink to show humour; a pat on the back is encouragement and a lick on the face is love. Following behind is loyalty and chasing after that is faithfulness. We learn by experiencing each other and sharing with each other. We are taught by observation, participation and involvement, and because we cannot rely on spoken language, we become more attentive and watchful. Silent communication requires patience and a readiness to understand.

In our human world when something seems to be beyond our grasp, we find ourselves speechless. People are too busy to know their inner thoughts and feelings, let alone finding words to describe them. Truly we are rather insufficient in our human communication, and we have begun to question true meanings of many words and sentences. With such consideration, it is only reasonable that we feel the need for fresh concepts and new vocabulary in our cross-species relationships. But too often we just have to revert to what we know best to describe our animals. It is then far too simplistic to define this as anthropomorphic when we haven't really found out the full complexity of dog consciousness. It is in such contemplation that I find our language inadequate, its limitation lying in our own human experience.

I do find it reassuring how other dog owners talk about their dogs' feelings, and even the vet says: 'See how your dog feels about it,' or 'He's depressed because you've been away for such a long time.' Max doesn't hide his feelings at all, he shows clearly how he feels about us, our behaviour towards him and our decisions regarding him. But how do I learn about how he feels? That is the real mystery, plus the fact that I have yet to find the right language to describe my observations.

What else can I use to describe my four-legged friend, if not human vocabulary? What I do know is, that just as you sometimes know how people feel when you observe it in their eyes, Max's big brown eyes can express his delight, excitement, joy and gratitude, his disappointment, sadness, fear and much more.

Yet while there is something lacking in the everyday expressions most people use to describe and explain their human–dog relationships, Mark Doty, in his book, *Dog Years*, uses his own creative language in describing his dogs. He tells about the 'sloppy dog way' in beautiful detail, saying that his dog is a 'vessel' carrying his will to live and giving him the power to move on. Doty's dog has become his life's focus and inspiration, and his extraordinary vocabulary for his feelings towards his dog goes beyond the reach of normal human comprehension. I believe that only 'crazy' dog lovers would know what Doty is talking about, and that only when you can truly feel the warmth of a pure gaze upon you will you know what it means to be given that power.

Yes, words too frequently fail us. I find I have thoughts and feelings about Max which are beyond description, less because of my own inadequacy but more because the very range of ideas requires a different set of qualifiers that are not available in human spoken language. Often we are compromised in our conversation because we have misunderstood something another person has said, or for the sake of simplicity we employ vague generalisations that we think may be more easily understood. It is commonly acknowledged that many problems in human relationships are the consequence of miscommunication and misunderstanding. If we could be as pure and transparent as dogs, we would perhaps not need a wider language to express ourselves and we might be able to reduce some of our relationship problems. The experience with dogs reveals to us the downside of our civilisation and sophistication, and points us to new dimensions of relating to one another.

You can sometimes know that someone is in love with you simply by an especially attentive look or some other non-verbal sign. In this case, your interpretation is not only based on the closeness of the relationship but also on intuition, experience and insight. The understanding between humans and their pets is similar. We do not need evidence for every-thing when our hearts can tell us what is happening.

By not relying on words we become 'doers', when our actions speak louder than our words and when, no matter how much we may talk, our actions still reveal the truth. Quite often Max watches me busily cooking or working at the computer when it's his usual time for the park. He never barks to ask me to go out with him, instead he just sits quietly next to me, exceptionally attentive and confident that his good behaviour is enough to remind me of his desire for pleasure. And I have never failed him; even when I am tired or sick, I don't neglect his needs. The power of love doesn't require us to talk.

As Doty points out, 'To choose to live with a dog is to agree to participate in a long process of interpretation.' This is very true as we are rarely given a clear message from our dogs.

So we interpret, which means we must be observant, sensitive and patient in order to find out about each other. With Max I often need to rely on guessing, yet somehow, most of the time, I just know I am right. This is a process that can't be gone through without mistakes, so we do have misunderstandings and are puzzled at times, and he does get confused, especially when one of the members of his family reacts unexpectedly or too strongly.

Dogs guess a lot, too, so they quickly pick up your meaning and their power of association is astonishing, but sometimes, when I wonder what Max is actually thinking or feeling, I really wish he could talk to me. I look at his face and his slightly parted mouth, trying very hard to convey a wordless message to me. At least he has found an easy way to express 'no' and 'no more': he simply sits down. When we go to the park we always make sure that he does his big business before we return home, and often, as we urge him to do it and he really has nothing to produce, he will just sit and look at us, telling us 'no more'. How very smart.

Of course, sounds are extremely important for dogs and I speak to Max constantly, usually slowly and clearly, singling out key words and repeating them. But there is no talk without listening, and ours is not a one-way communication; he listens all the time, never wanting to miss a sound. This requires the most faithful dedication, because constant effort is required of him in trying to understand, especially in our multi-lingual household. He understands both German and English, as my German husband speaks only German with him and I speak mostly English with a little bit of Chinese. When my husband is away and I need more authority to back up my commands, I might use a few of Max's familiar German phrases, small commands such as '*Du benimmst Dich gut*' (You behave yourself) or '*Abends trink nicht so viel Wasser*' (Don't drink so much water in the evening), in the hope that he will associate that language with his big boss and behave more obediently. I know that many dogs are able to follow spoken commands, but I have been told by my dog-loving friends that Max's ability of comprehension is exceptional.

Dogs can also distinguish meanings from different tones of voice and volumes of sounds, and even the way of talking can signify whether we mean real business or it's just a game. As a result of my softer, more easygoing attitude and sometimes inconsistent reactions to his demands, Max knows he can wait until I am really serious before following my orders and, just like a child, he constantly tests the limits of my patience. He has quickly learned how far he can go and who has the more compassionate heart, but when I raise my voice and speak firmly, he knows I have assumed the boss's role.

It is well known that dogs' ears pick up many more sounds than we humans can. This is why they know their master's coming home even before they arrive at the door. It seems amazing, then, that they don't seem to notice the sounds from a TV or radio—or maybe they do hear them but are smart enough to know that it is not 'real' sound since it has nothing to do with them. It's a true puzzle how the sound of gunshot or deafening rock music on TV doesn't seem to bother them, whereas a small animal moving quietly about the garden makes them go crazy.

Max barks only when necessary, which is to say, necessary in his own doggy needs. Whether he's trying to join in with the dog next door, replying to a call from a faraway friend or just alerting us to some strange happenings, he barks loud and clear. Of course, he barks fiercely whenever he hears the noise of an intruder, human or animal, even though it may be just a passer-by. In his old age, climbing the stairs is an effort that wears him out, so sitting on his own in the middle of the living room, he protests loudly at being left downstairs. His bark is a reminder of his existence and his desire to be with us.

In his youth Max would howl. Raising his head towards the sky, he would open his mouth wide and release a long, doleful sound like that of a wolf. It was quite mystical, usually under the silvery-yellow light of a full moon; spooky yet alluring. Now, when he crawls into bed after a long and tiring day and is about to fall asleep, he sighs deeply. And when he's excited or worried, he whines like a whingeing child. During periods of communal silence he will utter small sounds from time to time, just to reassure me that I am not alone. These all strengthen his presence at home.

Despite all this, in the end, Max's greatest mystery lies in his muteness, which floats, ungraspable, in the spaces between us. I almost want to pack up his silence and store it somewhere safe, to study in my own time what it means to not use words to talk to me.

## CHAPTER FOURTEEN

# BELONGING

A dog's lifelong goal is to belong, to be part of a community, to be ranked in a pack of either dogs or humans, and because of this innate conception, a dog in a home soon comes to know his place. We talk about stupid, unruly or untrainable dogs, but in the end, with the right handling, they can all find their appropriate positions. They may test the limits, play some tricks and attempt to upgrade their ranking, but ultimately they know they belong to us, that they are not free. Of course, there are always exceptions, and, just as in our human world, some dogs will fall through the cracks. This is especially pitiable for dogs as they come to know themselves by looking at their owners, as if by referring to their leaders they find their identities. Observe a dog looking anxiously for his master and you will know what 'at a loss' means.

Unlike humans, dogs do not yearn for freedom. They want consistency and wait for the same regular signs, sounds and directions. Max has always waited, to bond and be given instructions—although it is true that in his older age he often falls asleep during the wait. His waiting is a link from nothing to something, from inaction to action, from emptiness to meaning; it fills the gap and contributes substantively to our lives. A signal activates him, a simple signal without which his life would be purposeless. What must it be like, being owned and forever a follower? For humans it would be dreadful, but dogs enjoy and crave it, and are so ready to please that this must be part of their make-up.

When Max lies at leisure in our garden looking out at the water and up to the sky, I still can't quite comprehend how he came to be a part of our family. For he is not merely a physical presence with us, he is the embodiment of everything that constitutes family: closeness and connectedness.

In *The Philosopher's Dog*, Raimond Gaita says: '. . . it astonishes me that a dog should be part of our family'. In the same vein, I want to know whether Max ever feels strange that I should be his family. Other than the mistress who gives him food, cares for him and plays with him, what am I to him, really? The way he looks at me sometimes suggests that he too is puzzled over our relationship and how it could be possible— this existence that is not only functional and purposeful but meaningful as well. It frustrates me that I can never get into his head to find out.

Mark Doty describes the experience of living with dogs as a kind of 'domesticated wilderness', where humans can have a taste of the primitive and are constantly reminded of the far-off existence of a different world. I knew, when I saw how Max pinned down another dog in a few seconds or chased away street cats on a dark evening, that he actually belongs to the wild and that fighting, and perhaps even killing, are in his instincts. Living with dogs enables us to have this tenuous link to the wilderness. How much have our four-legs tamed themselves in order to be accepted by us? I believe we admire and adore our dogs because of their readiness to adjust themselves in order to fit into our human world.

And what else is there that makes dogs so appealing? We are charmed by their innocence, their vulnerability and their loyalty. These are qualities that are so often lacking in our human world. Gaita rightly points out that we are attracted by our dogs' 'otherness', that it is their difference, rather than any similarity, that enchants us. I see what I am not in Max. I know how much I want to unravel his mystery, not merely to understand the quality of being a dog, but more to make sense of what it means to be a four-legged animal following a two-legged human.

And does he assess me as a human? And what does he make of all our human activities that are such a big part of his life? There are times when, from his particularly fixed gaze, I'm sure he's thinking that the things I'm doing are unnecessary. Like when I'm dressing, putting on stockings and make-up, and I think I see bewilderment in his eyes, as if he's saying, 'Why do you bother?' Or when I'm impatiently rushing in and out of the house carrying heavy shopping bags, carelessly dropping things, or even worse, accidentally stepping on his paw, and he gives me a cold glance suggesting disapproval. At other times he is simply disappointed. Why then is he willing to take our orders? Is it because he thinks we need him and he's doing us a favour by being here for us?

We may attribute our authority to our higher intelligence, but in a dog's world it is physical strength that counts. So if Max doesn't see strength in me, why does he acknowledge my leadership, and what is it in me that subdues him? Our dogs' feelings for us are apparently not changed by what we do or how we act. They accept us as we are because of our role as their owners. They simply move into our lives and let us control theirs.

A dog that exists on its own is not fully alive; it should belong somewhere. So Charlie is sweet in the eyes of his owner, Lucy's faithfulness is known only by her master, Oscar is loving to his human parents but can be aggressive to everyone else, and Branda is beautiful to her owner even though she's really a strange-looking mixed breed. This doesn't mean that dogs do not possess objective attributes—they do—but the truth of those qualities matters only in relation to their owners, who find real meaning in words such as 'loving', 'loyal', 'sweet' and 'obedient'. I feel and understand what 'being sweet' means when Max comes close and licks my hand, and I see 'faith-fulness' in the eyes of a dog waiting for his master, eyes never moving from the shop door.

We give an identity to our dogs when we teach them to know us, and in doing so we give them the chance to teach us to know them. It is in this process that we are able to bond and understand the true meaning of loyalty and faithfulness. As Jeffrey Masson explains, loyalty is the desire to be together with a loved one—'to be where one belongs'.

Max has given me an identity. Not only am I his owner, I also belong to him and find myself in him. He reflects who I am and how I am. For Mark Doty, his dog and he were inte-grated into each other. It was through his dog standing by him that he was able to cope with life in its darkest moments. That is why, after his golden retriever had died, he still felt 'the quality of him, the aspect of him, most inscribed within me'. I understand what this means. As the years have gone by, I know there is a large and indispensable part inside Max that is me. And the part of him inside me is the purest and most delicate.

## CHAPTER FIFTEEN

# THE INTIMATE RELATIONSHIP

As Rudyard Kipling wrote: 'Amongst the many species, dogs stand out as our first friend.' It has been claimed that the ability to respond to and serve us comes from dogs' shared similarities with humans. In fact, many veterinarians talk about the similarities between people and their pets. In *Kindred Spirits*, Dr Allen Schoen writes: '. . . the more we study the differences between human and non-human animals, the more we see how similar we are.' The veterinarian and animal behaviourist Dr Nicholas Dodman, in his book, *If Only They Could Speak*, emphasises that other than sharing certain biological and genetic similarities 'it is the psychological resemblance that is so astonishing and fundamental to the interspecies connection'. There is no doubt that humans and dogs share a lot of sentiments, and dogs seem gifted with the ability to understand and identify with our happiness and sorrow. The poet and dog lover Pam Brown is right when she says: 'Humankind is drawn to dogs because they are so like ourselves—bumbling, affectionate, confused, easily disappointed, eager to be amused, grateful for kindness and the least attention.'

I could add another five or so human qualities that are commonly found in dogs, and then there are the dogs-only characteristics such as total loyalty, which complement human insufficiency and make our lives more interesting and rewarding. It seems to me that we, mankind and 'dog-kind', are meant for one another, made to complement and supplement each other.

Dr Patricia McConnell, another animal behaviourist, says in her inspiring book, *The Other End of the Leash*, '. . . humans and dogs are more alike than we are different.' I think the 'alikeness' refers to our ability to connect and click, to be linked with and tied to each other and to share feelings, due mainly to dogs' eagerness rather than any diligent attempt by humans. There is no doubt in my mind that it is because of dogs' unique sensitivity that we are able to connect so profoundly.

Dogs are all about feelings. They have plenty of them, all the time, generated by their acute senses, and the compelling fact is how they show their feelings so generously. This is beyond us, and therefore it never fails to touch our hearts. Their loving feelings for us are demonstrably the most important element of all in their relationships with us, and it is capable of causing an emotional revolution.

In his book, *Moral Questions*, Rush Rhees goes further, recognising that: 'I had come to know where I was with [my dog]. And each of us knew this.' Rhees later realised that he was 'kind of paralysed' by his dog's death, for 'I made no move without him'. As Raimond Gaita remarks, 'It is quite unbelievable how a dog can leave such an enormous impact on a human.' No wonder those who don't know dogs regard this life-changing impact with scepticism and tend to consider the 'changed' human to be emotionally imbalanced. What they don't know is that in the right circumstances, certain dogs can cause that kind of near-miraculous effect.

Many dog lovers believe that their dogs possess a life force that is able to stimulate, activate, energise and empower. Living with a dog, we are confronted with life itself and pushed along by the rituals of that existence. The loyalty, faithfulness and love of these animals make dog parents feel blessed in our cold, aloof and post-modern human world, for they are always there for us and eager to make us happy. Their naivety and resemblance to innocent children is so disarming that it allows us to feel and share this freedom and defencelessness. Their truthful characteristics demand no pretension on our part, we simply feel honoured by their honesty.

Dogs take you the way you are: whether bright or dumb, pretty or ugly, elderly or youthful, right or wrong, to them you are always good. They accept who you are and adore you all the same, never bearing a grudge or seeking revenge, for in their consciousness there is no bitterness. Yet they can feel much, and deeply, and there's never any mistaking whether your dog is happy or sad. In jubilation or sorrow they do not hide but show all they have: be it strength or weakness, their feelings are expressed directly and intensely. I feel relaxed, untangled and at the same time overwhelmed by the totality of truth presented by my dog in his simple way of expressing himself.

For responsible dog owners their dogs' complete dependence on them awakens a sense of obligation, and somehow they feel strengthened by this call to duty. I often remind myself that I am handling a life, not just a living thing, but something special and valuable as well. When we adopt a very young dog into our families, we witness their growing up and then growing old and getting sick, and at the end we are there with them for their final walk, to bid them farewell. There is no other relationship that enables us to experience this entire journey of life from beginning to end. We cannot see the childhood of our parents and our spouses, and generally we are not there to witness our children's growing really old. We rarely live with our siblings and friends in adulthood and besides, we are not responsible for their lives. But with our canine friends it's the whole process of life that we are dealing with, which is both a high duty and a noble task. Perhaps that's why we find so much meaning in our relationships with them.

I believe the reason we so easily fall in love with our dogs is because the close relationship is pure, truthful and without consequences. As Rush Rhees so rightly points out, we do not have to keep our distance with animals. A dog's feelings towards us are certainly real and true, and we can be sure that this love will never fade. Rather, the longer they are with us, the stronger and more intense the relationship becomes. There is no discouragement, no unfaithfulness, no wearing out. Even when we humans make mistakes or fail to fulfil our duties, our animal friends are not swayed in their dedication.

In human relationships we often consider how much gain or loss a nascent friendship may bring and we tend to distance ourselves when we feel incipient complications, or a danger of getting too close might make it difficult to break free. Then there is the constant worry that our admiration or love will not be returned or is being rejected. I suppose the frustration in a romantic human relationship is in the uncertainty of the feelings. Therefore the love we talk about between humans is often a calculated sentiment, a means for something else, such as security, pleasure or self-gratification. Some idealistic humans hope to lead a life of unconditional love only to be disillusioned, for human love seldom works in a one-way channel; it expects an abundant return or, at the very least, a balance. Giving, without getting something back, is considered stupid, but to a right-minded person, taking without giving back is just as unacceptable. That, perhaps, is why Jeffrey Masson dares to say: '. . . love for a dog is greater than any love between a man and a woman, for it is a completely voluntary and selfless love.' We give our love to our dogs without calculation, hardly expecting them to show us as much love in return. And of course they do and give much more than expected. They are the most generous lovers.

Rhees sums this up in a philosophical way when he says: 'The fact that it does not make sense to talk about sin in the case of animals is one reason why you can have closer affection there than you can have with humans.' Precisely: it is the imperfect human nature that obscures feelings, blocks the flow of emotions and makes pure love mostly impossible. Dogs don't negotiate, they are always ready to offer themselves because they don't know any alternative. In fact, theirs truly is blind love. In the realm of feelings, we humans surely still have a lot to experience and explore, and no creature other than dogs can show us more, clearer or deeper.

Masson regards the loving feelings of dogs as their essence of being. He writes: 'Dogs register no need to theorise about love . . . they just show it. And show it and show it and show it.' Masson's three dogs have shown him so much endless love that he claims 'that the dog *is* love, that dogs are all about love'.

Gaita, however, thinks the concept of 'unconditional love' is not rightly applicable to dogs, for they are not conscious of what they are offering, not to mention their unawareness of the possibility of 'conditions'. In this sense, their love is spontaneous, innate and something like instinctual.

Sometimes when you observe the behaviour of certain dog owners you know there aren't many reasons for them to be given a lot of love, yet their dogs love them dearly. It is a dog's instinct to bond and it seems that their desire to please has no selfish motive. They so eagerly enjoy the fun and joy of being in love, finding no reason to restrain their love. In my early years of living with Max I was often puzzled by this simple and direct love, and I thought perhaps it was because he wanted food from me. I soon found that he loved food, but he loved me more, for while he was eating his dinner he continued to check on me, and as soon as I left him to go to my room he would stop eating to follow me. It is an overpowering feeling to be loved in this doggy way and I don't believe humans are capable of such purity of sentiment. We have expectations and we set conditions on all aspects of our lives, but living with a dog can teach us to love for love's sake.

J.R. Ackerley, a former literary editor of a BBC magazine, writes in his book, *My Dog Tulip*, about how he often had to do a few rounds of walks near the train station to allow his Alsatian dog to relieve herself before their train trip to the country. This was indeed a tedious procedure, especially as his dog was very particular about finding the right scent to do her business and they would often miss several trains as a result. Many people would find it incredible that anyone should show such patience and loving care. And in his book, *Marley and Me*, John Grogan describes Marley as a messy, troublemaking, rather stupid and unruly dog, but he and his family accept him the way he is and love him deeply.

I've often wondered why people don't just give up on a troublesome dog and have concluded that they must never-theless be touched by the fixity of their dog's devotion. We humans learn a lot about love from dogs, and in our cohabi-tation we have become capable of loving them without conditions, not because they are a champion breed or a beauty queen and not because of their looks or their brains or what they can accomplish, but simply because they are as they are. It's a relationship not tainted by outward performance, hidden agenda, set goals or desired achievements. Their charm is naked, and we adore its nakedness, and in a paradoxical way it is their vulnerability that charms us as well, and because of this it calls for our good hearts to cherish and look after them.

Indeed, how we humans are delighted to offer protection and take control! Our dogs' dependence on us is one of the reasons why we are willing to sacrifice our time and energy for them. Dogs give us a unique sense of ourselves: in reference to them, we are conscious not only of our ability to take care of the vulnerable and be compassionate to the unfortunate but also of our authority and power as guardians of their world. It is clear that, being human, we can never be entirely selfless. Far from it, in fact, for we keep dogs at home at least as much for ourselves as for them.

Both Dodman and McConnell relate from their professional experience how humans benefit from the companionship and comfort of animals. The lonely or those who have had disheartening experiences in human companionship find being with and talking to their dogs or other animals much more rewarding. Even the socially successful recognise the beneficial effect their animal friends have on their wellbeing and they cherish the relationships. A number of studies and texts written on intimate human–animal relationships offer abundant evidence of the ability of animals to enrich people's lives.

## Chapter Sixteen

# OUR CREATURE WITHIN

I have recently come to recognise the 'creaturely nature' of humans. Raimond Gaita uses the term more in relation to the surface similarities of our behaviour with animals, but I see it as our suppressed playful desires, resembling that of the canine. Dogs, other than having to satisfy their basic needs, are much of the time playful, like children. Adult humans, other than fulfilling their basic needs, must also appear thoughtful and intelligent, so that many have lost the ability to play, laugh and be fully alive. It is when we mix with dogs that our 'creatureliness' surfaces, and we find ourselves coming down to the dogs' level, playing with balls, lying or rolling on the floor, chasing after one another, making ourselves dirty, and engaging in many other silly games. This is when we become our 'basic' selves and return to our infant mentality. I like to think, like Mark Doty, that dogs offer us a taste of wilderness, that there must be a part of us that actually rebels against the civilisation that has taken away from us our most real senses.

Interestingly, Patricia McConnell says: 'Dogs and people aren't normal mammals.' She points out that both species still love to play even at a mature age, whereas most other animals play games only when they are young. I believe this is why we say dogs have a transforming effect on humans: they rejuvenate, heal and enliven us. Through living with us, dogs draw out not only our rawest and crudest but also our deepest characteristics, unintentionally leading us to shed our human protective garments to return to our inherent tendency towards play and fun, doing it simply for the sake of enjoying our pets, with no subtle philosophy or grand theories.

Indeed life is also about playing a game, talking to an animal, chasing the birds, walking in the rain, sitting and staring, as well as working hard, thinking deeply, talking impressively and acting sensibly. Civilisation has robbed humans of simple merriment, and technological progress has moved us too quickly forward to be able to remember what straightforward pleasure is. Dogs' faces give you plenty of inspiration—the way their eyes glow, ears twitch, mouths smile or just open, panting with desire. We are interested, bewitched, and gradually we come out from our bondage of sophistication to be integrated into a state of sheer rawness with our animals.

While I do clearly see the difference between Max and

myself, I have become more and more aware of what bonds us together. A little action that makes him happy can keep me laughing uncontrollably, so why would I be so amused by this animal play if there were not some innate 'creaturely' quality inside me that responds to it? By joining in our dogs' activities, we forget that we are superior humans shaped by modern refinement, and by humbling ourselves to respond to this other species, and hence to our inner desires, we are able to find abundant pleasure in effortless ways.

## Chapter Seventeen

# WALKING

We live by time, with time and for time. We are a product of our past and we are unceasingly creating our future. We act and react in a process involving people, animals, things and events, with a purpose, a task and a goal. To live a human life is to embark on a mission with endless duties, worries, troubles and burdens, and sometimes miseries. Of course, we also experience excitement, satisfaction, happiness and joy, but it doesn't make sense to say we live a carefree life. Because of its very nature, our human life can never be free from care, for we are constrained by time and our awareness of it. No matter what we do, time runs away.

To be human is to be in a timeline, with our consciousness repeatedly being shifted back and forth. We remember and are shaped by our experiences of the past, even as we visualise and make plans for the future. That's why we can never truly relax and enjoy the present, and why some people try to forget time for a while by indulging in drinking and drugs. Despite what the positive-thinking gurus may advise, we can never live only for the present.

Dogs can take us away for a while from our human concerns and bring us to the moment, the now. Be it attending to them or taking them for a walk, they lead us away from our own preoccupations and suddenly we don't need to take action and manage the outcome. We truly feel free from having to achieve and accomplish. Jeffrey Masson talks to my heart when he writes: 'The dog opens a window into the delight of the moment, walking with a dog is to enter the world of the immediate.'

Dogs live in the present: for them this is what matters. Miseries of the past may have an effect but do not continue to press on them, and the possibility of misfortune in the future does not discourage them. Their way of smelling, looking around and checking things out points us to what is taking place now. Being with them and finding out what they are after make us more alert to what's going on, so that we, too, become more sensitive to and aware of changes around us. Dogs don't miss a sound, never lose sight of a strange event, can't let go of a special scent. For them, life exists in what draws their attention, and in those moments we forget ourselves, too, our baggage of the past and fear for the unpredictable future. In other words, they show us what it means to live without work and worries.

Mark Doty is right when he says: 'Walking with [my dog] is an affirmation of physical life. We're in the world, we're breathing, we're together.' Going for a walk is a daily activity, an essential part of living with a dog. It is the sign of life, the acting out of living, a movement that takes us from one point to another, both physically and metaphysically. Walking with Max has brought me into a new realm of existence. I see people and things I've never seen before, or may have seen but never really noticed; I actually feel that I live for the moment, and the feeling of being alive and well is real and reassuring.

Walking is a metaphor for consciousness: scenes change, people move, birds sing, eyes see, noses smell, ears listen, the mind works, the heart beats, and we follow life's path, moving ever forward. I am not surprised when I read about recent studies on the many benefits of walking for general wellbeing, especially in the prevention of Alzheimer's disease, and I thank Max for never failing to remind me to walk. Without him I would perhaps walk just for the sake of exercising my body, which is with a purpose, but walking for his sake is to take what comes along, to see and feel what is happening, to be there, witnessing the events of ordinary life.

Life itself is like walking: it is a chain of small excursions linked together to make one long journey. Soon after we are born we learn to walk, and once we have started we keep on going towards our unknown destination. This journey of life seems not to stop; even if physically we actually stop walking, life still moves on. This realisation of the continual flow of life is especially strong when I pick up my legs and walk my dog.

The heart sets a rhythm for our daily walks, all hustle and bustle put aside. I feel this time as belonging to me and my dog, what Doty calls 'extended consciousness'. It is when the two of us, inseparable, become one entity. Whether Max walks next to me, ahead of me or behind me, he is definitely there, standing by me, a companion and a friend as well as a clear and real physical support and comfort. Even though I may have weak legs, sore feet, a wearied heart, a heavy head or burdened shoulders, and I may fall, I know we will never desert each other and we will compel ourselves to finish the walk. So we keep lifting up our feet and paws and putting them down, as much in our daily walk as in life.

I also feel the joy of doing nothing when walking in Max's company and simply watching his physical being—his good-looking face and shiny coat, as he runs between the trees and in the long grass—for it is those moments when time seems to be standing still, when I feel like framing it and being captured in it with my dog. It's amazing how an animal can hold us from rushing into the future.

Walking is not time wasted. Far from it, it's a chance for reflection, recollection and review. I speak to God during our walks and I come close to the natural world. I am not just an outsider watching, I am absorbed and become part of it. As soon as I step out of the house I am more than an individual, I feel connected to and part of the whole of existence. There is something at work, something that takes me away from my own narrow mind and small body into a bigger and more encompassing realm, higher and more powerful, something that makes me feel joyous and complete. My Four-Legs and I are both inspired by the wind, the rain, the setting sun, the tumbling leaves and all that belongs to nature.

It seems pretty straightforward—going out to walk the dog—but when I return home I am light-hearted and renewed. I have fulfilled my responsibility of taking care of my dog's needs, and his happiness in return shows me that I am a good dog owner. To live with a dog is to take on the task of caring for a living thing whose very existence hinges on our sense of duty. The nobility of this sustains us and allows us to recognise our own importance. By carrying out our duties we know who we are and what we are capable of.

By going on our daily walks, Max and I take a break from everything else and enjoy our companionship. Other than his food, this is all he really asks from our relationship. Little can he know that over the years this simple request has made me a happier, and certainly healthier, person.

## CHAPTER EIGHTEEN

# THE SELF, LIFE AND THE SOUL

Our family will never be able to calculate how much love we owe to our Max, and he has no idea how significant he is in our lives. He has probably never thought about himself—and indeed, why would he, when his greatest wish, which is to be with us, had long since been granted?

Though far from being merely instinctive, dogs are far less self-conscious than humans, therefore they are more concentrated on whatever they are doing, smelling, seeing and hearing. They do not have secret agendas: if they want a treat they let you know, and if they don't get one they don't get angry. They have no ego to hurt. Some people may regard this as low intelligence or stupidity, but I think this 'selflessness' is in fact a virtue we humans are not able to achieve. Dogs don't spend time on themselves: if they are injured they don't fuss about it and they waste no energy indulging in self-pity. I have seen a three-legged dog happily running around with other dogs, and my old and weak dog continues to climb up the steps many times every day to be with us. Even bearing pain from his arthritis, Max still tries his best to chase away the cat intruder who visits our garden regularly. When he thinks he can be of use to us, he will just forget to protect his own wellbeing. Dogs' lack of self-awareness is what makes their devotion pure.

Where we humans differ enormously from animals is in our greater concern for ourselves. We can be self-pitying or angry with life, especially when we think we've been unfairly treated. We often question the meaning of life when we are confronted with frustrations, as if it consists solely of our personal success and happiness. We seldom take life as it really is without our fantasies and dreams, but Max demonstrates a grand theory in his life's simple activities—he acts out the very essence of life by participating in and living it. He tells me, 'Do not think so much about yourself, know where you are going, get up and go. Be playful and joyous.' How marvellous!

So, how significant are our canine friends to us? How far would we go to protect and care for them? My friend's daughter was working overseas when she applied for leave and flew back home just to be with her dog for the last days of his life. Her mother had already moved onto the floor to sleep next to him because he was too sick to make it onto her bed. I have heard of dog lovers spending thousands of dollars to treat their dogs' illnesses; even those who are short of money don't hesitate to pay large sums to save the lives of their beloved animals.

How much should we do just for a dog, and what is the limit? Should we do as much as we would do for our own children? At what point do we say our dog's life is less important than a human life? And how do we measure the importance of any life?

Every life means something, for no life exists completely on its own. It achieves little to compare different lives, for each life is unique and its value is known best to those who are touched by it. A dog's life makes sense in relation to its owner, who in turn finds meaning in their lives together. There is no universal touchstone we can use to decide whether the dog's life is worth keeping, except in the knowledge and feelings of the master. So when we ask 'Why all this, just for a dog?' we imply that a dog's life is of less significance, simply because it is an animal. If a dog is our best friend, loyal guard and loving companion, then the question should be 'Why not all this?' The answer would be much more straightforward: 'For my dog, who is my best friend, loyal guard and loving companion, I try my best to sustain his life and make it good.'

This is not a sign of weakness, nor is it because we are failures in our human relationships that we develop these close bonds with our animals. The reality is that many of those who are unable to maintain satisfactory human relationships are also unable to relate to animals, whereas animal lovers are generally kind-hearted and unselfish people who can readily express their emotions for others.

Nicholas Dodman considers that a close relationship with pets '. . . indicates loyalty, caring and strength of character. Understanding pet owners are better people than their animal-unfriendly counterparts.' For many dog lovers, their faithful dog friend may not be a substitute for their human friends, but the dog relationship may well be closer. I used to consider intense love for animals to be pathological, but now I know that deep love for a dog does not indicate a weird disposition, nor is it the outcome of failed human relationships or the salvation of a depressed soul. Most dog owners are positive, happy people who know what is significant in life and what makes life more interesting. As many veterinarians have observed, dogs can bring out the best in people.

Allen Schoen regards these sentient beings as like gifts from God. He calls them 'kindred spirits' and encourages us to treasure our time with them and to aim for a much deeper connection with them than simply taking them out for a walk or giving them food. He advocates a relationship of '. . . a co-mingling of the mind, body, and soul'. That our four-legged friends are capable of responding to our souls may in the first instance be incomprehensible, but almost every dog owner can feel how deeply their dogs can touch them, where understanding is beyond description. The soul is where our deep emotions and high virtues are developed and stored.

Jeffrey Masson, who is not religious, is convinced that 'there is some profound essence, something about being a dog, which corresponds to our notion of an inner soul'. Is it the total and true love that the dog is so ready to pour out to us? Is it because we can never quite comprehend the dog's acute sensitivity, the fact that he seems to know so much and yet remains so pure? If there is an uncontaminated spot inside us where we can bond instantly, then that, perhaps, is the soul.

It is beyond logic and reasoning, nothing that we can touch and grasp. I know it is in the air between Max and me, as if there were a thread tying our two souls together. As Anatole France puts it: 'Until one has loved an animal, a part of one's soul remains unawakened.' I have learned a lot from the nobility of my relationship with Max, although I cannot always apply those lessons in the human world where so many of us have contaminated, bruised and groaning souls. So it is a rapturous blessing to come across a 'kindred spirit' in the sometimes wearisome walk through life.

## CHAPTER NINETEEN

# THE MEANING AND BEAUTY OF LIFE

We humans will continue to have our hearts touched by the presence of our dogs, and to be intrigued, not only by their difference—how they move, play, show emotions and relate to us—but also by how we are so alike in our need to be together and to be loved, in all the simple happiness and sadness that make up such a large part of life. We are made to complement one another, to share and enjoy our various parts of creation together. I cannot imagine a world without animals, and I certainly haven't yet managed to contemplate how I'll live my life without my Max once he passes away.

We often take each other's existence for granted and miss the immediate significance of our coexistence. Why is there something instead of nothing? Why are there creatures other than humans? Why do we live with dogs? What is the meaning of inter-species communication, friendship and love? Every aspect of creation is a work of art that has a purpose and a meaning, and every living thing is a part of the whole. And the force behind every breath and movement, all the power and the majesty and all the glory that is nature is the Creator Himself.

When I look at Max I see a work of creation, feel the essence of life and seem to understand the meaning of his existence for me. Yet I do not really understand how this being, created in a totally different form and image, can be my dearest friend. Although I do not know why he is made to have four legs, I cannot hide how much I admire the beauty of that wet nose, the saliva hanging from his big pink tongue and, of course, the ears that can be squeezed.

I check Max's ears, eyes, nose and thick coat again, and wonder what we mean by beauty. What should I admire in those four skinny legs, furry body with its bushy tail and funny face with its big black mouth so full of huge sharp teeth? And the strange nose, with its many little smelling dots, why was he created this way to have that incredible ability to identify millions of scents? If the whole of creation is beautiful, where lies the beauty here? It is clear that I see my dog as extraordinarily attractive—his handsome face and uniquely coloured coat make him outstanding—but I cannot help pondering on the application of the term 'handsome' to dogs, a word we normally apply to humans. What is handsome in an animal? Everyone says about Max: 'What a beautiful dog,' yet surely they all have their own view of what is beauty? So what do they all see?

The concept of beauty is a subjective individual appreciation. There are, however, certain qualities we all agree to be beautiful. I often sit and watch Max from different angles, noticing how his nose sits between his eyes and mouth and how he puts his tail around his body when he's lying down. I see him yawn, redirect his ears, shake his body and wag his tail. Yes, indeed, I find him so beautiful. Everything about him is beauty, even when he barks and chases the cat.

We say something is beautiful when its form and shape are pleasing to the eye, yet it is character and nature—goodness—that constitutes true beauty. True beauty is found in honesty, loyalty, faithfulness, truthfulness, purity, simplicity and, especially, love. That is why we don't hesitate to proclaim the beauty of dogs but are slower to identify human beauty, which can sometimes be tainted by characteristics such as arrogance and malice.

Beauty is found in simple ways, it lingers and belongs to the soul. An ugly-looking dog is still a beautiful creature. Such beauty transcends circumstances. I am overwhelmed by the power of beauty. It makes being alive a privilege.

Humans are seldom content with just their own affairs. Our curiosity drives us to discover what is not within us. We search for new knowledge and investigate the unknown in our world. It's almost our instinct to want to know other creatures, for their difference is our fantasy. Dogs' passion for humans can greatly satisfy our needs, and when we easily find happiness in them, we know that we have come across a masterpiece of creation. It is not through the working of the mind, but rather the understanding of our hearts that we reckon our connection with dogs to be an uplifting experience. This realisation rests outside the rational, and it is precisely why our relationship with them is so beautiful.

I see God's creation in Max's beauty, and I see the beauty of God in him. Animals, but especially dogs, lead us away from our human concerns and point us to something beyond. They are 'the other', they make us contemplate the mysterious, the higher and the more powerful, and they help us to think and feel deeply.

I am beguiled by what I am not able to grasp, and by how I could be so transformed by a single animal. I am open to new possibilities, and have learned to recognise simple truths and subtle wisdom. My bond with Max has heightened my awareness of the meaning of life, and because of this I believe we can soften and refine humanity.

# A TIME FOR REFLECTION

## CHAPTER TWENTY

# OUR TENTH ANNIVERSARY

A lthough spring had officially started, this was still a rather chilly end to a very long winter. I felt cold in the biting wind, shuddered, and breathed out warm air onto my hands. Then I noticed the fallen leaves churning in front of you, Max, and the piles on the ground, brown against the green grass field. I was so absorbed that I lost my sense of surroundings. 'Where am I?' I asked myself. I picked up a leaf and stroked it with my fingers, feeling its lifelessness. I turned my head to look at you, and seemed to feel your warmth upon my heart though you were standing on the other side of the park. Many nights after my operation, while I lay shivering in my sleep, you came quietly in to check on me, and in the dark you delivered a 'pawful' of care to my bed. In the morning I would see anxiety between your brows. Today was my first celebratory return to the park. I was delighted to be back and grateful to be alive and well. With your cheerful look you told me we should be grateful for life again.

I dropped the leaf in my hand, tightened the scarf around my neck and put my arms around my chest, almost laughing. I had survived this hard, cold season of my life. What happened now seemed almost like an ancient story, except that it was also so real. I had you and you made my story special.

You were there in your waiting posture now, as the day yielded to the scheme of time. I could see you, filtered through the trees, with the setting sunlight falling unevenly onto your golden orange coat in glittering patches, illuminating your body.

You paused and turned your head in my direction, looking for me. Your eyesight was still very good and I was certain you saw me. A golden retriever was walking past and a bull-terrier was rolling on the grass behind you, but you stood motionless, looking over to my side of the park with anticipation. I couldn't see your face, but from your stance I sensed some tension, as if you were worried you had lost me. The golden retriever moved towards you to check your scent, and I seemed to hear his owner admiring your sparkling coat, as they always did. But you remained still.

In that instant I saw you once again as the statue I had seen ten years earlier, but this time you were a symbol of life and a witness to many poignant moments. In one eternal second you were framed in my mind and stamped on my heart, and I knew I would never forget this vision of you posing among the trees. With that ray of sunlight falling on you it was as if you were carrying some divine purpose on that beautiful late afternoon in the park. It was 9 September 2009, our tenth anniversary.

From this distance you looked like a wolf standing firmly in the wild, proudly a part of it. I wondered how you could have been tamed to follow my orders. I knew you so well, but had I actually come close to seeing your real self? Caught a glimpse of you before domestication? I was enchanted.

However, it also seemed to me that you were far away, in another realm, in a world that I didn't really know. I fixed my gaze, but you were now just a vision, slightly blurred, at once expanding and receding in time. I couldn't believe my eyes anymore, you seemed to stand apart from reality. You were not in my grip and I no longer knew you. I realised that you didn't actually belong to me, that you belonged somewhere I would never know. You were just on loan to me for a while, so that one day perhaps, when your strength had passed on to me, I would be able to stand securely on my own in this new land I was still adjusting to.

Then I saw you trotting towards me and I waved at you, as other dogs started playing and chasing, in a display of energy and spirit. Your furry body was ruffled against the wind. The weight of your four paws was firm and steady on the ground, as they had been on my life. Over the wind I could hear the crisp sound of your steps in the dry leaves: it rang in my ears and startled my heart. On your four legs and with your bushy tail erect, you were crossing over the species barrier to come to my side.

Then you quickened your steps, preparing yourself for that long jump. You were a life force, and I didn't want to take my eyes off you. You had taught me to treasure our moments together. You always helped me to put the grand theory into practice.

I looked again and caught your eye. You were standing in front of me, holding up your head and staring at me with your usual inquisitive look, asking me: 'Why don't we go home? It's getting late and it's cold.' You always knew when to wake me up, whether from my sleep or my imaginings, never too early and never too late. I had become used to your speechless commands. And, of course, you were hungry.

Darkness silently seeped through the air. I could no longer make you out. Like the other dogs leaving the park, you also jumped into the car, and lay down. In the mirror I could just see your two big ears and large round eyes: they were like two dark discs, and I could still see them sparkle; ten years of life together had not diminished their charm; they could still cast a spell. Those eyes, from which support, encourage-ment, love and care poured out, day after day, year after year. The eyes I'd first seen at the RSPCA that had captivated me. Nothing could compare to them. I knew I would always see their charm and feel their sparkle upon me, even when they were gone from me. Even then.

The evening descended as we drove away and said goodbye to the park . . . until it all but disappeared. The night creatures were creeping out now that the last dog had left. We heard the wind making its rounds and I knew that more brown leaves would be falling. You didn't make a sound. I somehow felt your mood.

This had been just another of our twice-daily outings to the park, a routine we performed with an almost religious zealotry. Together we had notched up ten years of shared time, and now we were moving on to our bonus time. I stopped the car and looked back at where we had come from, asking myself, where had all those outings gone? Even in my memory, the events of the last ten years had begun to fade. I wanted to catch them and put them in a box to keep forever, but gradually one by one, they were evaporating. I wonder how much you can remember.

Back home, and this tenth-anniversary night belonged to just the two of us. We sat side by side and shared a piece of steak, and I didn't forget to give you a brisket bone. Outside was a world of fast changes, and we looked into the darkness. Out of nowhere came a roaring sound, and you stood up facing the glass door, barking fiercely. The dark sky was illuminated by a shudder of white lightning and then came the rain, like buckets of water pouring onto the glass door. A storm fulfilled. You were secure with me next to you. You rested your head on my lap, and I saw your frown and a slight melancholy in your eyes. What were you worried about? Could you read my mind, and understand my reflections?

You looked up at me and asked: 'What can we do about this storm?' And then you searched my heart, as you always do. No, my dear friend, there is nothing we can do about the storm. And it will be over, sooner or later: like everything else, it will also pass.

The rain eased, so I opened the terrace door and a gust of wind slapped my face. Then you led me out and taught me how to dance in the rain. I touched my wet clothes and your fur, to know it was real. I knew I might get a cold, but then I thought, if I could survive a four-hour operation, this is something I shouldn't mind. You brought me a tiny stick and we played throwing and catching. Your devotion warmed me up instantly.

Somewhere out there, perhaps, some serious meetings of life were taking place, but for this moment it didn't matter. Witnessed only by the stormy night, we indulged ourselves in this little fun. You made me laugh. You always know what is best for me. I felt the serenity around me, the peace in my heart, and I no longer had the fear and worry. From that moment on I let go and freed myself. I might not be able to accomplish my goals, but at least I had achieved peace.

## CHAPTER TWENTY-ONE

# TIMES OF
# OUR LIFE

I don't know how much you still remember of your RSPCA days or even of the two years before you came to live with us. I'm sure you never look back, as you have no need to reminisce about your past, although sometimes you do look quite capable of thinking about it.

Unlike humans, you animals live only for the present, for you are not conscious of the effect of time. You belong to a timeless realm where the impact of the past and the uncertainty of the future do not prohibit you from enjoying the here and now. I seldom look back, not because there was no glory then but because with you in my life my past has become irrelevant. I haven't stopped daydreaming entirely. I can't help fantasising about what might have been, but because I do not look forward to a future without you I don't want to cause myself unwanted anxiety by picturing how my life will be. So I have adopted your approach: we live day by day, together taking charge of the present. We shouldn't miss the past or worry about the future—at least that's what we try to do, don't we?

Yet the future is not for us to manage. After our tenth anniversary, I told myself that I should start preparing for changes in my life. You know how I always like to organise things well in advance in order not to be shocked by any unexpected events. I can still see your critical expression as I collected your hair, one ball at a time, to fill a cushion for myself. I let you smell it, and you looked at me quizzically, as if to say: 'Hey, woman, why be stupid and keep my hair in this little bag? You can see I shed heaps every day. Why are you doing this? I am right here carrying millions of hairs!'

Indeed, you have now been with me for almost thirteen years, but those years have been like water flowing down a drain and disappearing faster than I could imagine. Gone. Like my broken pearl necklace. Even before I'd realised what had happened, the pearls scattered to be lost forever. I stood there, bewildered and stunned by their sudden loss.

I once thought that life with you would be long and dreary and I would joke about how I was bored to misery by the tedious and unpleasant tasks involved in looking after you, like picking up your poo, cleaning and washing you, dressing your wounds, dropping the pills into your mouth, cleaning the soiled carpet and brushing your double fur when you only wanted to play. That was what I thought at the beginning, and how I laugh at myself now. As your faithful mistress, I have become an expert in most of those duties. The only thing I still require is your encouragement for our early morning outings in the chill of winter.

I have little time to think seriously about the breadth of our relationship. When I do find space to ponder on our life together, I only get a glimpse at what it has been. What I do know is that this journey has transformed my sense of existence.

Looking at you now, I am reminded of what has made me love you so much. I regret that I never made notes of my special moments with you. Of course, there were so many and I was always too busy, but I will always be touched by how you have strengthened and inspired me, how you have brought me so much peace and joy.

I do not want to believe that fourteen and a half years is already a lifetime for you canines, and that you have already outlived most of your contemporaries. I hesitate to acknowledge that the final phase of our life together has started, but your intense look keeps telling me that you don't want to part with me. Your devoted attention to me seems to suggest that we are running out of our time together. And then I have to accept it's not just the years that will pass, living things will vanish, too.

Last year you sat in my daughter's room and watched her pack up her belongings. You saw me carry her mattress out to the car and you witnessed our goodbye kiss as she drove away in pursuit of independence. You followed me back into her now empty room as I looked around and tucked her chair under the desk. You looked into my face to see if I was sad and I saw how you felt about losing your 'little sister'.

I wonder how you remember those times when only you could share her secrets and only she was allowed to hug you tightly. I know you can see for yourself that she has not just grown taller and bigger, but that she's no longer the little child she was when you first came. When she decided to move out, my first response was 'But what about Max?' I wasn't thinking about being left mostly on my own; I was concerned about how you would cope with her absence, knowing how much you love her.

As it has happened, almost every evening you take a little stroll to her room, comforting yourself with her scent. The room is already dark and the windows are closed, and the smell of her books, papers, bags, clothes and perhaps also her shampoo still linger in the space. Often you come out without a sound and quite unexpectedly meet me in the corridor when I, too, am about to pay a short visit. In the dim light from outside the window, we pause and say good evening. You follow me back down the hallway, watching me turn off the light and lock the doors. Silently we wrap up the day and spread out into the night. In the dark, your eyes still follow me. You never let me feel alone. And you share my feelings, discreetly and respectfully. Only you can.

And when my daughter comes home for a meal or weekend

stay, you make yourself silly pacing here and there to welcome her. It is as if she was just that innocent little girl for whom you had to find a toy or play a game. I watch how happy you are together. And every time she leaves again, you are puzzled and saddened. You just lie down in a corner, quietly accepting the changes in life.

I know you put on a show for me, too, and I am mystified by how you can know so much about human psychology. Why do you bother to be so interested in and excited about us even now, in your aging condition, when you could just lie around like most other old dogs? Why doesn't your passion vanish and why does your love never die? Yes, you are that little fire starter that lights the flame of emotion in our family.

I also know that you are forever waiting for your big boss to return home. You don't understand, of course, why he is always on the move when you think home is the best place in the world. It is a celebration every time he returns, but I see how you shut yourself down and plunge into sorrow when he packs his bags again. I don't think my husband understands how deeply you feel about the separation, for he has never witnessed your grief.

It is not only you who is perplexed. I also find it hard to accept how time has changed us. It always takes charge, and we can never stay the same. And then it starts again, and we may or may not be part of it. What has been becomes nothing, and what is new is not what we have known.

I can see you want to tease me again: 'Hey, woman, what philosophy is this? I care only for this time and my life with you.' Yes, this time, and all the experiences that have made it. Remember that fall into Sydney Harbour? What a big shock to all of us, knowing you were afraid of water. You must have been so thankful when my daughter, who was then just a little girl of ten, risked her life by climbing over the wall to pull you up, with my husband holding her from behind so that she wouldn't also fall in. And you must not forget our holiday with you—that almost three-hour drive was not pleasant for you, but how we enjoyed spending time together as a family for a few days! Every night after dinner we strolled slowly back to our cottage under a dark sky illuminated by millions of stars, you leading the way. We forgot about our human plans and goals and, for a moment, enjoyed the simple fun as a family.

I miss those carefree and playful moments, and I am saddened by the loss of them. Life consists of many comings and goings, and every one of them is a reminder of the transience of life. We are forever baffled by the many question marks in our lives as we try to live happily. You, of course, do not agree to many of our human affairs, and probably think that people are unnecessarily thoughtful. But, through you, I can hold on to the essence of life for a little while. I am the witness of your journey, and you are accompanying me on mine.

You do know what I am talking about, don't you? Do you know that the times of our life are precious and that one day they will all be gone? You spare me a laugh, turning your back to me, resting your face on your paws, deep in thought.

## CHAPTER TWENTY-TWO

# AGING, DYING AND DEATH

Last week I came across a lovely photo of you and Uncle Sam. Both of you were standing in front of the 'Million Paws Walk' banner in Centennial Park, displaying a cheerful spirit. You look young and very slim, a puppy face gleaming with vitality turned towards the older Uncle Sam, whose laughing eyes are looking at the camera, bright and clear. That must have been your first year with us and we were eager for you to socialise with other dogs. You soon developed a special fondness for Uncle Sam and kept giving him kisses whenever his owner brought him along to visit us. Some years ago, Uncle Sam passed away unexpectedly. When we visited his owner a week later, you became very restless when you couldn't find him. As soon as you ran into the flat, you detected something unusual, and you searched every corner and sniffed Uncle Sam's toys, food, blankets and towels. Then you checked the scent of the owner, looked at her and woofed as if you were questioning her about the disappearance of your dear friend. You turned your puzzled face to me, demanding my response. I, of course, had no answer for you because I, too, was rather baffled by the sudden change from 'being there' to 'nowhere to be found'. The room was full of Uncle Sam, only he was no longer there. You became very quiet and curled up next to your friend's bed.

On our way home, I told you that Uncle Sam had gone to Heaven. You didn't bother to question me further, maybe knowing this was not a topic normally discussed. You soon seemed to accept that Uncle Sam would never come back, and comforted yourself with his scent in his owner's home. This is perhaps why you decided not to befriend her new dog, Char-Char, although you see her every now and then when her owner comes to visit us. By ignoring her, is this your way of being faithful to your old friend?

At that time you were still quite young and strong with boundless energy. Now that we both have aged, we can perhaps talk about life's greatest mystery. I suppose you know what I am talking about, as you move unsteadily towards me, sensing my unusual mood. Your throat makes a worrying sound and you sit down to gasp for air, looking worn-out by our afternoon walk. As much as I understand that aging is inevitable, I find it hard to accept that you are sometimes feeble and delicate, and that you are getting sick, weak and will die.

You know how much I dread that one day we cannot avoid. Whenever you lick or scratch your body you stop as soon as you notice I am watching, and you give me your serious face, telling me: 'Hey, woman, don't overburden yourself. Can't you relax? It's only a little lump. Am I not able to handle my own body?' You try to look unworried, but what you are actually doing is hiding the spots and sores and lumps you have. You don't want to worry me. What instinct is this?

You lie down on your side, spreading your legs, eyes half closed, ready to doze. Even your ears are relaxed, and I can see the tip of your tongue poking out at the corner of your mouth, something that never happened when you were younger. It is a symptom of old age we have found in you only recently. This is not just an afternoon nap, you are now fast asleep during most of your time at home. You no longer wake up to greet us at the door when we come home, a sign of your degenerating hearing. The other day I came home after a long meeting, concerned that you might have been bored after being left alone for so long. Instead, I found you sleeping soundly on the floor. I put down my handbag and sat next to you and enjoyed the sight of you entirely at rest. Your eyes twitched and your legs shuddered. I watched your breathing, in and out, soft and beautiful. I wanted to hold you tightly, but I didn't want to disturb you. Then all of a sudden you opened your eyes. You were recovering from your dream and felt a bit embarrassed to find me beside you, not having been greeted on returning home, and watching you when you were unaware of anything around you. You surely want to continue to be alert and useful, I understand my faithful friend.

Your old age is clear and unapologetic. It has arrived fast and mercilessly. We mortal beings like to prepare ourselves for the final moment. Our cat Mimi found a quiet corner in the kitchen to pass away in the middle of the night. Will you, too, think of how you would like to die, or are dogs perhaps less 'intricate' than cats and don't really care how they go? Are you conscious that we shall soon have to part?

These days your face is showing your advanced age. You had a puppy face for such a long time and even early last year you could pass as a youngster in the park. Now I can clearly see greyish white hair underneath your eyes, above your nose and around your muzzle, and your lower chin is almost completely white. Although your body looks good for your age and your coat still shines, your back aches and your knees hurt. You walk with stiff legs and unsteady steps. You have had one accident after another. A few years ago we found a lump on your leg and they put you on the operating table. Out came the lump, and so did the five stitches that you took out with your still sharp teeth. I found blood seeping out of the open wound, so off we went to the vet again, this time for staples. Then two years ago you had a knee injury in the park and now your right leg is weak and you need regular injections. You don't fight anymore, although you cannot hide your fear. You now sit quietly and let me deal with your problems. Watching you, I know it is more than the pain, it is also fear of the unknown, the darkening of life.

But what bothers you most is your constant diarrhoea. I still remember how shocked I was when I first found your droppings on the carpet shortly after you came to live with us. I thought it was an accident, but over the years I have become used to your congenital weakness and quite ready to deal with it. It has always been a problem, but with increasing age, you seem to have lost control of your bowel movements altogether. Just a few days ago, you got up in the morning and were terrified to find your droppings underneath you. Now, in your deep sleep, things happen. As you fail to give warning, and at times are unaware of your own condition, I find myself spending more and more time cleaning up after you. While I work quietly, you lie miserably opposite me, awfully sorry for the trouble you have caused me. I ask myself: When is it enough? Where do we draw the line? When do I decide that I cannot cope anymore? Do we just accept the pleasurable and reject the troublesome? And what do we do with humans? Send them to nursing homes?

But I seem to have made my decision. I won't give up as long as you don't give up. So, my dear, it hinges on you. We shall work together to keep enjoying our life. No matter how hard. It will not be forever, anyway.

For some time I've noticed that you do take care of yourself. At almost fifteen years of age, you pull your legs along, limp occasionally, and sometimes slide. You slow down your movements, avoid close contact with your younger and stronger dogs, detour around rugged patches in the street and no longer run or jump to catch your ball. Your brisk, precise and energetic movements have gone; you know when it's too much and when you should let go.

Mortality does mean something to you. You sniff frail dogs with caution, careful not to push them down, and as soon as you smell death or old age you back quietly away. Once you dashed across to confront a bird that, to your surprise, didn't fly away. You were startled by its injury and looked at me with bewilderment, quickly leaving the poor creature in peace.

You surely know quite a bit about life and death, especially having had your own experience of the in-between, when you were struck down by a stroke that left you unable to walk or stand properly. As you were struggling to make sense of this sudden collapse, I rushed back from Hong Kong in shock and with a torn heart, expecting the worst. 'Well, he's a very old dog, such incidents are common,' the specialist said. 'Try these anti-stroke tablets, hopefully they will keep him alive for a few more months.' You survived the stroke, and now, although you are a lot slower, you are enjoying the bonus time that God has given you.

Miraculously, we continue to venture out for a walk every two or three days, but we have to pause from time to time for you to regain your strength. We both know this is import-ant exercise and that these moments are precious. So you happily struggle on, although sometimes you do need a bit of encouragement. Tired and slow, you drop your head, avoiding eye contact with me, embarrassed, at your clumsiness. Then you usually turn your head towards home. Your bushy tail now hangs down nervously between your legs to stabilise your balance. Your head is slightly tilted and your right paw is too unsteady to stand firmly on the ground so you limp a bit. I can see your collar sitting uncomfortably on your neck, tight where the loose skin has sagged to form a little pocket underneath your still handsome face. I'm sorry to say that you look a bit funny now, with your round furry body supported by four skinny legs, uncertain that you can complete the walk but not wanting to give up. I do understand your dilemma: your spirit hasn't been broken by the stroke, but your body feels the weight of each heavy step. I wonder, should I urge you to keep going or should I just let you go?

I put my mouth close to your ear and say, 'Come on, good boy, just a bit more walking and we'll see your doggy friends in the park.' You usually need a few seconds to think it over and you search my face to find the assurance of our long companionship before you step forward. I walk beside you, clearing the fallen twigs that may trip you and paying attention to cars that may come dashing out of the driveways. So we pace our steps and enjoy another lovely outing together.

Sometimes in the park you put your age and all its bothers behind you, as you quicken your steps, focus your eyes and raise your tail, turning around quite swiftly, to say a big hello to your buddies. In these moments you seem to also forget the pain. When you do fall down, you always make an effort to get up again and enjoy being alive. I cannot hold back my tears: how I would love to see you active and strong again.

Getting into the car has become a real challenge as you are no longer able to jump. You have also lost quite a bit of your sense of spacial recognition. For some time you would try to jump up from a wrong angle so that you'd bump your legs on the side of the car or on the bumper bar. I was really terrified by this, but I couldn't help as you were far too heavy for me to lift up. So I found you a ramp. Do you remember that strange box-shaped thing? It gave you quite a shock when it opened and you were stubbornly determined not to use it despite the many delicious treats I offered you. When your big boss came back, he found a sturdy ramp and trained you to use it, and to my surprise, to please him, you walked bravely up it and into the car.

This is a huge departure from your energetic past. You certainly didn't like the ramp at first, but soon you realised it was the only way to get into the car. Now you have accepted the new arrangement and don't mind about the tedious procedure involved in setting it up.

But you haven't forgotten your duty of guarding our house and you still like to demonstrate your faithfulness, especially when your big boss is around. The other day, while he was enjoying a quiet afternoon in the garden, those annoying ducks flew in to have a swim in our pool. I saw you pull your weak legs across the garden to chase them away, and as you turned your head to see if he was pleased with your effort, I heard my husband praise you. Did that make you happy, that you were still of use to him? You had strained your legs again, and watching you limp slowly back to the kitchen to have a drink, my heart ached for you.

Perhaps you thought this would impress your big boss so

much that he'd stay longer with us. How sweet your naivety is. In your old age you seem to cherish even more the little time you have with him. You gaze upon him with more than obedience and loyalty; you show concern about him, how life is treating him and how he lives his life. You understand that perhaps we humans also have our weaknesses. You think, just by being here, you can please us.

I'd rather not see you push your body too often or too hard, for after a while you shiver and your long tongue hangs out, you pant hard and your eyes bulge out as though it's an effort for you to remain alive. The other day you bumped against a door and almost fell down the stairs. I now apologise for embarrassing you by saying loudly for everyone to hear: 'Oh, you old boy, look how clumsy you've become.' Your big boss thought I shouldn't have reminded you of your age.

But who isn't worried about aging? I look at myself in the mirror and see more grey hairs. My legs now get tired more quickly and I find my shopping bags getting heavier and heavier. I, too, am dealing with aches here and pains there. Last year I had a really nasty fall and seriously bruised my back. I'd thought I would always be active and fast, but lying in bed suffering from excruciating pain I came to accept the fragility of life and I was terrified at the thought of how depressed you would be if I were to die before you. I'd rather you go first and let me mourn you. Your German Nana has just turned 93 and has forgotten a lot of things, but she still asks about you. I don't know who of you will go first, and when I think about it I become rather sad.

My own mother doesn't hide her fear of death, she shows it to me every time I visit her in Hong Kong. She's now a frail woman in her eighties who has lost her desire to live. The 'spirit' is no longer to be found in her, but I cannot even ask her how she would like to be buried, for she would be furious at the possible bad omen associated with the word. Many humans complain about the meaninglessness of life, but they also cringe at its transience, whereas you animals are superior in this respect. You take life the way it is and do not carry unnecessary worries. When the time comes you just let go, is that not true?

Because we only live once, I am not able to accept the fact that whenever I leave you I might not be able to see and touch you again. This remarkable relationship I have with you happens only once in a lifetime. Whenever I leave Sydney there is a heaviness in my heart, for something might happen to you while I am away, especially now that you are so old. You probably understand when you see me pack my bags with a sad face and from the hug I give you before I leave home that my departure may mean our permanent separation. Usually I pull your face towards my chest and stroke your cheeks—my attempt to take a bit of you with me. And then I quietly weep for leaving you behind, knowing how much you will miss me. I know you wait for me by the door every day while I'm away.

Now I hold your face and squeeze your ears as if I can capture your DNA so I might have you forever. You yawn widely, tilt your head and eye me intently, making sure I'm not out of my mind. Then you roll over, dancing with your four legs in the air, rubbing your ears on the floor, turning from side to side, demonstrating just how alive you still are. You cute, silly thing. They all say I should get a new dog after you have gone, but they don't know my feelings for you and they don't understand our relationship. No, not a new dog. Not a dog for company. You are irreplaceable. Only you can give me a real life force and a lasting love, and I shall be faithful to you.

It's easy to understand that I have rather mixed feelings about your inevitable death. I am quite prepared for the day, whenever that may be, but I don't want it to come, not so soon, not this year or next year . . . I do know a little about death.

My father died during a visit to a foreign land, in cruelly cold Toronto. I didn't see him die, he went into a coma after a stroke and was gone before I arrived. I remember my heart froze as the first snow of that year fell, and in the long silence, I didn't know how to grieve. My father had been healthy and strong, and I felt that he just disappeared. It was only when I finally began to cry that I knew for sure that he no longer existed and I would never be able to see him again. I kept thinking: 'How did my father die? What was in his mind?' And now I can't help thinking: 'Oh, Maxi, how will you die? What will be in your mind?'

What does it mean to go into lifelessness and complete silence, to be breathless and cold? What leaves the body that it can no longer move? Where does the being go before disappearing without a trace? Max, your death will take away from me not just your physical body, but also your wisdom, spirit, force of life, sense of joy and song of love. You will leave me with a vacuum, and the huge task of refilling my life.

Now in your sleep you move your legs—they seem so full of energy—and then you fall again into stillness, but only for a minute. You must be running after the ball in your dreams. I watch life expand and fade. I will not live to see my daughter's old age. I didn't know my parents or my husband as children. But with you, I have witnessed the cycle of life. Images of you, young and blooming, are still fresh in my mind. I hope I will be there by your side for our moment of farewell. I have made a vow to accompany you on your last steps, so please don't go suddenly when I am not by your side. Please wait for me to comfort you.

But mentally you are still very strong and far from ready to let go. You often cast a jolly look at me, wanting to share the secret of bliss. Although there are now some old-age obsessions, I still admire your spirit. After a long nap, you will pull yourself together to play with the ball or your magic duckie. Your eyes still gleam with excitement at the idea of going for an outing. As long as you can get up, you do, and you do so with dignity and enthusiasm, always ready for the wonders of another day.

You know you are old, but you don't act old; you still stir when you see the cheeky little dogs in the park. Only the other day I had to remind you how unfit you are now for a buddy play fight. Of course you came to your senses, and turned your back on those energetic youngsters. Your tired paws slid slowly towards the car. You'd had enough and wanted to go home.

I have learned from you, my dear loyal old comrade, that it matters little how long or short life is. What is truly important is the quality of life, and that life depends on what we put into it and how we deal with its challenges. Although you are often tired and weak, you continue to offer your pure love and care. You have given me your fighting spirit, and joy of being alive.

The weight of your head on my lap, the smell of dog fur in your blanket, the moisture of your nose on my finger after I have held your face, your smelly and dirty stuffed toys, the marks of your previous droppings on the carpet, all have one meaning to me: being alive, being joyous. You are the *constant*, from the beginning until the end. I am no longer afraid of the dark. After you have gone, I know you will always be there for me. I am truly grateful to you.

Will I know from your big brown eyes when it is the time for you to go? You must let me know when you no longer have a desire to live. Will there be a time when I have to make a decision to end your life? I know you won't want to leave me on my own, so how can I then do such a thing against your will? Or will you be given that fatal needle so you can have a painless and peaceful death? I check your face now and keep asking myself what I should do.

In the end, I know you will be true to yourself, but the when and how will be left to me. I have provided you with a rich and full life, and now I'll be responsible for determining when and how it will end. I don't want you to suffer, so will you give me a signal when the time has come and you can no longer endure the pain? I dread that moment when I'll have to make the ultimate decision. That moment of no return.

Aging and dying: a journey of endurance, and courage, and wisdom. Do you agree with me, my Four-Legs?

## CHAPTER TWENTY-THREE

# THE MEANING OF YOU

You come over, pant a hello and sit down opposite me, honouring our pact with all your heart. These days I often feel the intensity of your eyes on me. You are not just being inquisitive, but are examining my soul, demanding answers of me, searching out my dreams. I know you probably don't approve of them because you think this experience with you should be enough to make me content. Whenever I am unsettled, you offer me your warmth and tenderness. Your caring melts my heart.

You are so much more than just a dog. It is in you that love and faithfulness all culminate. At times I want so much to know what it's like to be you; not just the dog, but the unique, adorable, smart and funny being who can read my mind and who stole my heart, this best friend of mine who loves and cares for me. You have opened your heart to me. How blessed we are, for we truly have each other.

The other day a guide dog and his blind mistress walked past me, and I couldn't take my eyes away from that beautiful dog. His head was raised as he looked forward, not distracted by anything. His firm and erect body, carried by his four strong legs, was proudly ready to perform his most meaningful duty. The word 'noble' flashed in my mind. I stopped walking and turned my head to continue looking at him. His steps were steady and confident, and as he moved he radiated dedication. His mistress trustingly allowed herself to be led. I saw as she patted and talked to him, how obviously very grateful she was to her dog. My eyes swelled with tears. I understood well that this was a very private moment between two sincere hearts. That day I came home with even more appreciation for dogs. I remember how every time you saw a guide dog, you would move aside or turn quietly in another direction. You didn't want to look at it or disturb it in any way. The first time I noticed this, I found it quite unbelievable that as young and as fun-seeking as you were, you were also sensitive to and understood the importance of that dog's duty.

Honourable is what dogs are. You serve with dignity and without reservation. You love but without demands. You are humble and you are immensely responsible. When I see your dedication and your faithfulness, I am ashamed of our human selfishness.

Goethe said: 'We are shaped and fashioned by what we love.' I wonder how much we two have been shaped and fashioned by one another. I know, in the deepest sense, that you don't actually exist without me, that your true meaning is to be found in your relationship with me. You probably don't realise how much we have both changed.

From the beginning your innate good nature was the excellent handiwork of God, but our experience together has brought this out even more. In a way, you have become more than human because, unlike us, you cannot learn selfishness.

At the same time you have challenged me to expand my own narrow vision, and in doing so have transformed me, opening my eyes to a new world of wonder. You have shown me my strengths and weaknesses, and you have seen me at my best fighting battles of the soul and mind. You were there when I fell and when I got up again. You have led me to know what a simple and good life is, and the joy of living it. With you, my energy and spirit just soar, simply because your own are so contagious.

Now you lie on your side, falling asleep while trying your best to keep your eyes half open so that you may still be aware of my existence. My presence has become so important to you: if you cannot find me, you become very unsettled. Sometimes, in the early morning when you first wake up, you pull your weak legs over to my bedside to see me. Feeling secure, you fall asleep again next to my bed. I am not sure whether you are worried about yourself now that you are so old and frail, or if you are concerned about me. Yes, we two are an odd pair. Looking back I know that I would not have been able to cope so well with my new life in this country without you. I owe you now for the life you have given me. Thank you, my Maxi boy.

I do not want to finish my book thinking about what my life will be like without you. I know right now that I should enjoy every bit of our time together and be forever grateful for you, my marvellous blessing and my wondrous gift from God. He hasn't just lent me His shoulder to lean on, He has given me four more legs.

You, meanwhile, continue to examine my soul. Your big brown eyes speak louder than ever as they gaze steadily at me. You have much to say to me, as always.

# EPILOGUE

It was a bright early afternoon, clear and still, an ordinary autumn day that would pass by like any other. I checked the sky for the third time and imagined that all of a sudden the grey clouds would come and rain would start to fall. I said to myself, 'It would be right that the rain should come now . . .' Dark sky. Pouring rain. Isn't this the way it should be? I heard the doorbell and at once froze. My daughter went quickly upstairs and opened the door. In special moments she's always the smarter one.

As the vet and the nurse walked into the room, I pulled the skin around my finger nails so hard that it hurt. Max moved his legs a bit. I was taken aback. How calm he was lying there on the floor mat, how strong and brave. Perhaps he did understand what I meant when earlier I had told him what the vet would do and that he would go to Heaven, where he would run around again. We stared deeply into each other's soul, and when I said goodbye, he lifted his face. Then he dropped his eyes and put down his head. He never moved again.

I felt unreal, as if I had been captured in a movie that would replay itself over and over in the years to come. I had rehearsed this moment in my mind many times. It wasn't a surprise, but my heart was hollowed and dripping: the needle that went into Max's leg had sucked it out. No rehearsal could prepare me for the pain, the searing pain. I fell into a depth I had never known.

Later a man came to collect Max's body. I saw my Four-Legs being put on the stretcher, carried up the stairs and into the van. His face was at peace, like he was in a deep sleep. So beautiful. An image of him in the park came back to me. I thought perhaps he'd just go for a while; perhaps tomorrow he'd come back and wake me up from this nightmare, and I'd see him again . . . Then the man shut the door of his van and said 'I'm sorry', as if he had contributed to Max's departure. I watched the van drive away with my Four-Legs.

Max passed away on 2 May 2013 at 1.15 pm after a sudden outbreak of infections in his elderly body. For three days he had refused to eat, strong minded as usual, true to himself in the end.

Max left me four months after I had completed his book and four months before it was due to be published. I have kept the last part of my book in the present tense; I do not want to change it to the past tense. There are certain things that are meant to be, and should stay the way they were.

I never knew there were so many tears inside my small body, but when they all poured out, I was left dry and aching in mind and heart. There is now an emptiness to confront. It is agonising not to be able to see, hear and touch Max like before. Missing him is an understatement. I have discovered a new capacity to feel.

Grief is a solitary journey. It's quite ruthless and relentless, all-consuming and overpowering, but at times it can be surprisingly fulfilling and even inspiring. I have finally received my grief, and learned to accept it. I am going through it, taking my time, tasting it and dealing with it, gently and creatively. It's a time, I now realise, when I am closest to God, who gives and also takes. It's humbling to be in sorrow, but the enduring experience with Max is so sustaining. I still hear his four legs trotting behind me wherever I go. Didn't he always tell me that he would still take care of me even when I couldn't see him?

In this book, Max is the beginning and the end. He has completed his walk. He didn't cheat or quit halfway. I started my new Australian journey with him and his passing made its end. I suppose I should now pick up the pieces of my dripping heart, restore them, and start anew, with his book.

Thank you very much for reading this story. It was because I knew you would care that I had the courage and persistence to write it.

*Do not stay at home and cry.*
*I am not there, I will not come back.*
*I am the gentle breeze that strolls by in the morning,*
*I am the autumn rain that drips from the leaves,*
*I am the full moon that gives light to the darkness,*
*I am the vast ocean that releases power for your soul.*
*I am the look of tenderness, taste of sweetness,*
*I am the smell of comradeship, sound of friendship.*

*Do not lie in bed and weep.*
*I am not there, I will not get you up.*
*I am found across the park and beyond,*
*I am seen through the happiness and the sorrow,*
*I am heard from the lapping waves and flying seagulls,*
*I am felt in the soft air and the warm sun.*
*I am the reason for joy, wish for blessings,*
*I am the vessel for love, message for meaning.*

*Do not be mistaken,*
*I have gone, but I am still around.*

—Max, 3 May 2013

# ACKNOWLEDGEMENTS

The motivating force for writing this book was my wonderful four-legged best friend—my greatest thanks should go to him. But it was my husband who chose Max at the RSPCA, and my daughter who insisted that he was the best dog. I am truly indebted to them for adopting Max, so he and I could develop our extraordinary relationship. I must also point out their unfailing encouragement of me during the process of writing this book. Thank you, my family.

But this story would have remained just my personal pleasure without the committed support and guidance from my mentor, Diana Giese, of the NSW Writers' Centre. I thank her very much for believing in me as a writer, and I especially appreciate her valuable suggestions and advice to me in preparing the manuscript for submission to agents and publishers. Diana, I am very grateful for your help, you switched on a bright light for me in my journey of writing.

My dear friend, Beverley Burke, who has many years' experience in editing, was the first one who read the whole manuscript and reviewed the story. I was fortunate to have her to discuss my work with, and she taught me to be critical of my writing. Beverley, many thanks for your contribution.

The published book owes much to a special lady who was instrumental to its birth—my agent, Selwa Anthony. I was touched by Selwa's readiness to represent my book and indeed impressed by her exceptional professional style, coloured with thoughtfulness and enthusiasm. She is also a passionate dog lover with whom I could relate right away and share my feelings about Max. Selwa, I am very blessed to have you as my excellent and caring agent. You have my utmost appreciation. I cannot thank you enough.

I would also like to thank all my friends who were concerned about and loved Max, in particular Nell and Rebekah, who showed me selfless love for dogs. Similarly, I cannot overlook the efforts of the Rose Bay Veterinary Hospital in caring for Max, enabling him to live a long and happy life with us. Dr Howard, Dr Michael and Dr Jude, you are remarkable vets. We admire your professionalism and kindness very much. I must also acknowledge the wonderful treatments given to Max after his strokes by the animal physiotherapist Kristine Edwards and animal acupuncturist Rae Hennessy.

Kristine and Rae, you both contributed to helping Max live his last months with less pain and more fun. Many thanks.

Naturally I am obliged to my publisher, Allen & Unwin. It was an unexpectedly pleasant journey to publication. My deep gratitude goes to Rebecca Kaiser, the Editorial Director, who valued my story, sold it to her colleagues, and allowed it to reach the public. Rebecca, thank you very much. It goes without saying that I am very grateful to the editor of my book, Alex Nahlous.

# REFERENCES

Abramson, Neil, *Unsaid*, Centre Street, New York, 2012.

Ackerley J.R., *My Dog Tulip*, New York Review of Books, New York, 1999.

Dodman, Nicholas H., *If Only They Could Speak*, W.W. Norton, New York, 2008.

Doty, Mark, *Dog Years*, Harper Collins, London, 2003.

Drewe, Roberts, *Walking Ella*, Viking (The Penguin Group), Melbourne, 2006.

Gaita, Raimond, *The Philosopher's Dog*, Text Publishing, Melbourne, 2002.

Grogan, John, *Marley and Me*, HarperCollins, New York, 2005.

Horowitz, Alexandra, *Inside of a Dog*, Simon & Schuster, New York, 2012.

Layton Robin, *A Letter to My Dog*, Hodder Moa, New Zealand, 2012.

Masson, Jeffrey, *Dogs Never Lie About Love*, Vintage, London, 1998.

Mayle, Pater, *A Dog's Life*, Penguin Books, London, 1996.

McConnell, Patricia B., *The Other End of the Leash*, Bantam, 2002.

Rhees, Rush, *Moral Questions*, Macmillan Press, London, 1999.

Schoen, Allen M., *Kindred Spirits*, Random House, Australia, 2001.

Thomas, Elizabeth Marshall, *The Hidden Life of Dogs*, Houghton Mifflin, Boston, 1993.